Don't just dea
about it COM
AXID DC

SEA FISHING

SEA FISHING

Trevor Housby

BLANDFORD PRESS
Poole   Dorset

*First Published in the U.K. 1983 by
Blandford Press, Link House, West Street,
Poole, Dorset, BH15 1LL.*

Copyright © 1983 Blandford Books Ltd.

*Distributed in the United States by
Sterling Publishing Co., Inc.,
2 Park Avenue, New York, N.Y. 10016.*

British Library Cataloguing in Publication Data

Housby, Trevor
  Sea fishing.
  1. Saltwater fishing
  I. Title
  799.1'2   SH457

ISBN 0 7137 1225 2

*Phototypeset by Oliver Burridge and
Company Ltd, Crawley, Sussex*

*Printed by South China Printing Co.
Hong Kong*

Contents

To my son Russel James,
may he enjoy fishing
as much as I do.

Introduction

Sea angling has become an extremely popular sport in recent years. Overcrowded river banks, industrial pollution, the high cost of club fees and of bait, all these have led to a massive upsurge in sea angling as a sport. This new interest means that many tackle developments have taken place and sea anglers are now specialists rather than just anglers. Make no mistake, sea fishing may have its problems but, by and large, there are still plenty of fish to give good sport throughout the year.

Sea angling is a year-round sport. There are no close seasons of the kind found in coarse and game-fishing circles; the fish are seasonal in themselves. Mackerel, for example, come in late May and stay until the end of September. Cod arrive in October and leave during early February. Many species overlap so far as seasons are concerned, but to get the utmost out of each year you will be well advised to learn and understand as much as possible about the movement, habitat and general likes and dislikes of the fish you intend to catch. By studying the various factors involved, it is more than possible to increase both the size and quantity of your catch. The old days of 'chuck-and-chance' are long gone. The modern angler sets out to catch a particular species and uses and needs modern methods and tackle to achieve this aim. Fish are far from stupid. They live in a highly-competitive world where food is at a premium and where one mistake can cost the fish its life. Fortunately, modern tackle is extremely advanced and most fishing-tackle companies strive to develop better and more efficient tackle. Good fishing tackle is not cheap; and to fish properly several varied sets of tackle are required. It is possible to keep up to date with tackle development and technique by reading the angling papers on a regular basis. This is important. Far too many anglers learn the basic principles of angling and then forget or can't be bothered to study the constant up-grading of ideas. Anglers who belong to sea-angling clubs which hold competitions on a regular basis usually keep up to date on new ideas and, although competition angling is not everyone's idea of sport, a season or two spent studying the local club champions and fishing against them in competitions will often give an extra edge to an angler's basic skills.

Fishing should be fun, however, and to become too competition-minded can sometimes spoil the basic pleasure of angling as a sport. Use competitions to improve your fish-catching skills, and then apply these skills to everyday fishing. In this way you will get the best out of sea angling.

Bass

The bass is an unmistakable fish. Even anglers who have never seen one in the flesh will have little trouble identifying the first specimen they catch. The bass belongs to the perch family and, like its freshwater cousin, has a large spiny dorsal fin. Its neat, extremely compact body is covered with hard, firmly attached scales, which give the fish a rugged yet streamlined appearance. Bass, particularly small bass, vary in colour from bluish-grey to greenish-grey on the back, with brilliantly burnished silver flanks and white underparts. Very large bass sometimes have dusky grey backs and rather tarnished silver sides. A bass in prime condition is muscular and heavy shouldered, with a hard head and huge mouth, obviously well suited to a hard life in rough water.

Most rod-caught bass range from 2-6 lb (0.9-2.7 kg). A fish weighing over 12 lb (5.4 kg) can be looked upon as an outstanding specimen. The largest bass yet caught on rod and line in the British Isles tipped the scales at over 18 lb (8.2 kg). Monsters of this calibre are, however, extremely rare and are becoming rarer with each season. There is evidence that, under favourable conditions, bass can reach weights of well over 20 lb (9.1 kg).

Unfortunately, sea anglers have been slow to realise the value of conservation. Bass, which are slow growing, are among those species seriously depleted by over-fishing both on a sporting and on a commercial basis. This has become particularly true during the past few seasons when inflated prices have been paid for bass by European fish buyers. Commercial fishermen and anglers have been quick to smell a profit and as a result bass have been virtually wiped out on many of their traditional feeding grounds. Facts and figures are always hard to establish but figures of over 20,000 lb per boat for a single day have been recorded. This is

9

particularly true of West Country waters, where local fishing boats would go out of business without bass.

If there is to be a future for bass, it is essential that the club anglers and individual anglers set themselves a limit and adhere to it at all times. Unfortunately, few anglers follow this principle, and those who take vast hauls of bass, justify their mass destruction of priceless breeding stock by stating that the fish they catch are a drop in the ocean in comparison to the shoals that still exist. This may be true but if nothing is done soon to stop the slaughter, the species will be harried to extinction.

The Splaugh rock, off southern Ireland and the Eddystone reef off Plymouth are typical examples of the dangers of over fishing a particular area. Once the most famous bass grounds in the British Isles, they now produce very little. The once-huge bass shoals, which were decimated almost daily, are a thing of the past and it is very doubtful whether they will ever return. This is **not** an overstatement. Careful scientific investigation has shown that bass are a slow-growing species: a 10 lb (4.5 kg) bass may be anything up to 14 or 15 years of age. Fortunately, at this stage, it will have hopefully spawned successfully at least once and this, to a degree, makes it expendable. The problem lies, not with the killing of extra-large fish but with the mass destruction of thousands of immature bass which never have an opportunity to reproduce. Go to any fishmonger and, sooner or later, you will see immature bass on sale. By ministry standards these fish are above the legal limit, a fact that proves the uselessness of a size limit which makes it perfectly legal to destroy fish which are too young to breed.

At some time or another, every bass addict has been guilty of killing a large number of fish. I know I have. But as soon as I realised I could not dispose of the majority of my catch, I acknowledged the stupidity of bringing home fish I could not use or give away, and promptly stopped the practice. Now I only retain fish for which I know I can find a use. Obviously, this doesn't mean that I stop fishing the moment I have taken my self-imposed limit of bass but it does mean that I set myself a higher standard and immediately return fish under that standard to the sea. Far too many anglers get blood lust when fish are biting freely, and kill everything they catch without a thought for the fish or future seasons. Worse still, anglers have discovered that small bass make first-class live bait, with the result that bass stocks are being depleted to supply bait for tope fishing. This practice, which is frowned upon by fishery authorities and club officials alike, should be banned and, in my opinion, anglers found guilty of using live or dead bass to catch tope or any other large predator should be expelled from their angling club or penalised by the Fishery Board.

In the British Isles bass can be caught from the Suffolk coast round to the Welsh coast, becoming more and more common as you go to the south. Bass probably have a far wider distribution than most people realise; bass have been taken from the west coast of Scotland, particularly in Luce Bay, during the past few seasons and it would seem likely that regular fishing in this and similar areas of the Scottish coastline would prove that bass frequent the northern waters in a far greater quantity than has been supposed. The south and north coasts of Devon and Cornwall provide wonderful bass fishing, as do marks on the west coast of Wales. In Irish waters, bass fishing is often superb.

In my own area, the marks around the Isle of Wight produce very big bass. For example, a boat fisherman live baiting in Alum Bay caught a monster fish weighing $16\frac{3}{4}$ lb (7.5 kg) and the bridge off the Needles Lighthouse is often thick with bass of all sizes. The shingles in Christchurch Bay are often alive with very big bass and the run at the mouth of Poole Harbour in Dorset can be relied upon to produce several double-figure specimens each season. In the West Country large estuaries are favourite venues with men who specialise in small-boat fishing for large bass. The Dart, Teign, Fowey, Exe, Tamar and Fal river estuaries are all first-class bass grounds but I suppose the Fowey is the most famous West Country bass river.

During the past few seasons the east coast from the Thames estuary round to the Suffolk coast has become noted for the number of large bass it has produced. Ports like Bradwell-on-Sea have become established as big-bass venues with boats leaving each day to fish the offshore banks where big bass congregate in large numbers. Fortunately, conservation is practised by both skippers and anglers alike. Probably because the east coast is new to bass fishing and has learned from the mistakes of others.

Bass are attracted by fresh or brackish water and there have been many instances of individual fish, usually large ones, making long up-river journeys. On the Arun River in Sussex, very big bass were once caught on dace livebaits intended for pike.

Basically, bass are a rough-water species which thrive in heavy seas and in areas subjected to tide rips or overfalls. Rocks and reefs which cause the sea to churn and foam are ideal places to hunt for bass, and the rougher the water the better the chance of catching good-sized fish.

Any surge of water will attract bass. A small sandy beach, flanked by rock, often makes a great shore-fishing venue. In Ireland and Wales, long open storm-beaches are favourite places for the shore angler to try for bass. Harbours and piers certainly attract big bass; these fish are usually scavengers; they will hunt actively for small fish or prawns round stone or iron-work, but the majority of their food is gleaned from the sea bed. In commercial ports where trash fish and waste bait is often dumped from fishing boats, fish or squid strip make good bait.

At Dover, local night-anglers catch good bass on dead baits which float on the surface. The favourite bait is pouting. A plentiful species, whose swim bladder inflates if the fish is pulled rapidly from deep water. The Dover anglers simply push a hook through the pouting's tail, cast it out without float or lead and leave it to float on the surface. The hunting bass rise to this bait like a trout to a fly.

Although bass *can* be caught any time of the year, the effective bass-fishing season lasts from the middle of April until early October. During very-mild winters, bass in West Country waters may stay throughout the winter months as well but, as a rule, the first onset of wintry weather drives the fish into deep water away from the coast. In my experience the best bass-fishing months are May and June and September and October.

Bass in calm waters or estuaries often show their whereabouts by cruising on the surface with their backs and spiky dorsal fin showing above the water. This also occurs when bass shoals are working over bait fish like herring, sprat or mackerel fry. At sea, feeding bass shoals can be pin-pointed by watching for bird activity; as the bass drive the bait fish towards the surface, gulls and terns will gather to take advantage of an easy meal. Terns are, in fact, the most reliable guide to the whereabouts of a feeding bass shoal, although the activity of high-diving gannets has also led me to some good bass fishing. When the surface is broken by a number of heavy splashy rises you have a sure sign that bass are hunting. The splashes are invariably caused by bass rushing at bait fish which have been herded to the top of the water. Bass are predators by inclination, but they will accept practically any bait an angler cares to use. I have caught bass on squid, fish strip, whole live and dead fish, crabs (hard and soft), kipper, slipper limpet, edible clams, mussels, scallops, marine worms, sea mice, prawns, sandeels and a wide variety of fish fry. Even a small bass has a large mouth and, as a rule, big baits are the most effective.

Tackle

Boat-fishing tackle

Although bass can be caught on standard boat gear, the real bass specialist usually employs much lighter tackle. For example, when general bottom fishing from a boat a 12 or 20 lb (5.4 or 9.1 kg) boat rod should be used in conjunction with a small centre-pin or multiplier reel loaded with line of a 12 or 20 lb (5.4 or 9.1 kg) breaking strain. This same outfit can be used for light trolling from a slowly moving boat. For drift fishing, float fishing and spinning a lighter tackle should be used. My choice would be a glass, carp or salmon spinning rod, a medium sized fixed-spool reel and 12 lb (5.4 kg) breaking-strain monofilament. With tackle of this type, every size-able bass will be able to give a good account of itself. When hooked on light tackle, the bass is a real rough-and-tumble tearaway fighter which gives even the most skilful of anglers a run for his money. A landing net should be carried at all times. Gaffs should not be used when landing bass. Where possible, each fish should be netted, so that it suffers as little damage as possible. Unwanted fish can then be unhooked with the minimum amount of handling and returned alive and unharmed to the sea. If a gaff must be used, only use it to boat the larger fish.

Smaller fish should be shaken off the hook while they are still in the water. This is easy to do, simply take a firm hold on the hook shank and shake it out of the fish's mouth.

Shore-fishing tackle

Shore fishing for bass has attracted the attention of many dedicated anglers. Each will argue as to which rod or reel to use; and seldom will two such anglers agree. This can be confusing to a newcomer. To simplify the situation, let me say right away that *any* beach-casting outfit can be used to catch bass. The ideal rod, however, is (in my opinion) an 11 ft (3.3 m) two piece capable of casting leads of up to 4 oz (0.11 kg) in weight. This type of rod is versatile enough to use in all beach bass-fishing situations and as such is the ideal tool for the novice bass angler. Later, when personal experience dictates, rod styles can be changed to match individual requirements. This type of rod will comfortably handle lines between 14-20 lb (6.3-9.1) breaking strain. Choice of reel is, once again, up to the individual. At one time, most bass anglers vehemently believed it was wrong to use anything but a multiplying reel. Fortunately, reel snobs are now not so much in evidence. The secret is to use a reel with which you feel comfortable. Bear in mind that bass fishing from the shore is often a night-time occupation, so if you find a multiplier difficult to handle, settle for a good fixed-spool reel, as even experts experience overruns (birds nests) with multiplying reels. This can be trouble enough in daylight but at night it can be a disaster. Overruns are virtually impossible with a fixed-spool reel, where the spool of the reel remains stationary during casting. The disadvantage of the fixed-spool reel comes when fishing in drifting weed. A great heap of weed on the line can be difficult to retrieve with a fixed-spool reel; with a multiplier the weed can be cranked ashore quickly and easily.

Methods (Shore)

Spinning

For the energetic angler who likes to cover a good deal of ground, one of the most effective methods to use is spinning. Armed with only a light rod, reel, haversack to hold spare tackle, flask and some food, the spin angler can make his or her way from one likely spot to the next, covering a large area of water *en route*.

All sizes of bass respond well to artificial baits and even on days when the bottom fishermen find it hard to catch fish, the spinning rod will account for bass. I do not pretend that spinning is always the best method to use; in this country little serious spinning has been done, despite the obvious effectiveness of the technique, but those anglers who do spin from beach, rock, pier or jetty do report good sport.

Artificial baits are legion and it is easy to overspend when purchasing new lures. Many anglers become avid collectors of these things and habitually carry a vast selection of brightly coloured baits which they seldom use. To avoid becoming a collector, it is advisable to limit one's choice of lures so that only a practical selection is carried. Spinning round weed-covered rocks is at best a costly business, at worst prohibitive and even the most experienced angler must be prepared to lose a few baits during the course of an average day. Because of this, only the less expensive lures should be employed.

There are many suitable lures available and, where bass are concerned, the larger and flashier the bait is, the better it seems to work. Long Swedish wobbling spoons and plain pike spoons (see Fig. 1) are firm favourites with knowledgeable bass anglers.

(Fig. 1)

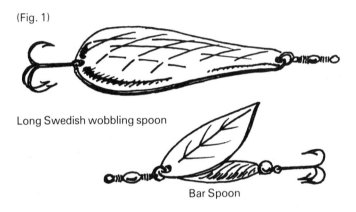

Long Swedish wobbling spoon

Bar Spoon

Some of the elongated solid lures from Scandinavia are good. They cast well, have a good action and certainly catch fish. Single and jointed plugs (see Fig. 2) make good baits but are expensive and have a tendency to snag up. Blue and white coloured plugs make the best baits; the best type of plug being a slow sinker. Plug baits are made in three types. *Floaters* which are designed to work on the surface. *Fast sinkers* which sink rapidly and *slow sinkers* which, as their name implies, drop slowly towards the sea bed. The Abu company of Sweden make a plug called a *Hi-Lo*, which has an adjustable diving vane that can be used to alter the depth at which the plug bait will work. These are highly effective but expensive. The Abu Rapala lures are also good. These are light-weight baits constructed from balsawood covered in a protective plastic skin. Rapala lures are world famous as fish catchers. For bass fishing the magnum-pattern Rapala is best. Rubber or plastic eels have always been a top spinning bait. The best and most refined pattern being the red-gill eel. There is a wide range of plastic prawns, crabs, squid, etc, on the market but these are designed to catch anglers more than fish and are best left alone.

(Fig. 2)

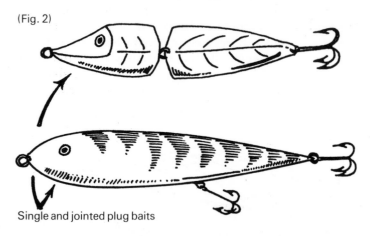

Single and jointed plug baits

For short range work it is seldom necessary to add any form of lead weight to the terminal tackle. With light tackle the weight of the bait will be sufficient for casting purposes. When extra-long casting is called for, a supplementary weight can be added; the cheapest and simplest being a plain barrel-lead, stopped at either end by a large soft split shot (see Fig. 3) or leger stop. This should be positioned 12-18 in (30-45 cm) from the bait. Although bass obviously hunt close to the sea bed, they seem to prefer an artificial bait when it is worked at midwater.

(Fig. 3)

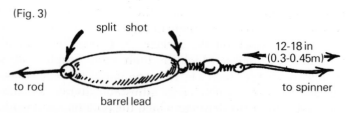

A barrel lead can be used to add weight to light tackle

To do this properly, the bait should be retrieved at a steady even pace. The rod tip can be swung steadily from side to side to vary the movement of the lure, so that the lure does not follow too straight a line. Plugs should be worked in jerks so that they follow a zig-zag up-and-down path (see Fig. 4).

(Fig. 4)

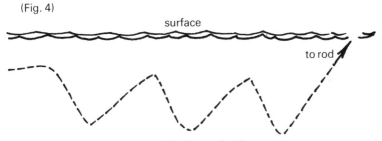

A plug bait should be retrieved in zig-zag fashion

Hungry bass usually take bait in a savage fashion, often hooking themselves in the process. There are occasions, however, when the fish will follow the bait without attempting to attack it. This can be most frustrating, as it usually occurs on a bright and windless day when the sea is calm enough for the following bass to be clearly seen. The only way I have ever found to tempt fish when they are in this finicky mood is to change to a very tiny bright bait of the Mepps bar-spoon type. This will often do the trick, although fish may be lost on the strike when the small hooks fail to engage. As mentioned, bass love rough water and it pays to spin the most-disturbed areas as thoroughly as possible.

Fly fishing

For the trout or salmon angler who wishes to try his hand at sea fishing, bass make a good starter. Salmon or reservoir-type lures used with conventional fly tackle can produce excellent results. Fly casting in salt water may be a new sport for Britain but it is highly effective.

Float fishing

One of the most rewarding ways of taking bass is to float fish from rocks which are surrounded by fairly deep water. Bass find a great deal of natural food in these places and good catches can often be made by presenting a natural bait on float tackle close to the rock face. One of the worst traits of the modern angler is his constant desire to cast further than his neighbour. The blame for this can be laid on the fixed-spool reel which is so simple to use that even a complete novice can throw a long line without preliminary practice. The ability to cast further than someone else does not necessarily lead to larger catches, indeed, where bass are concerned, it is often advisable just to swing the tackle out a few yards/metres. Otherwise, it is easy to overshoot the likely feeding areas.

Live prawns make excellent bait for bass fishing, particularly when light floats are used. Fortunately, excellent sea floats are now available, although my advice is to avoid the really large patterns and to stick to the more streamlined floats. Do not neglect to look for seawater floats in the freshwater section of your tackle shop. Many excellent floats, designed originally for pike fishing, can be adapted for use as saltwater floats (see Fig. 5). Except under special circumstances, fixed floats are seldom of much use to a sea angler. The best pattern, the balsa pencil, is made up with wire rings so that it slides freely on the line. Bass feed at all depths but it is best to set a float so that the bait is suspended at or around the mid-water mark. This is particularly important when prawns or worms are used as bait; if these are presented too close to the bottom, then the ever-present wrasse will find them long before bass come on the scene. Fish strip baits (see Fig. 6) can also be used on float tackle but these standby baits seldom produce such good results.

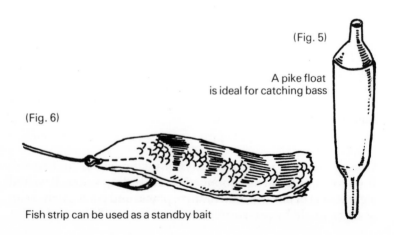

(Fig. 5)

A pike float
is ideal for catching bass

(Fig. 6)

Fish strip can be used as a standby bait

In the West Country, where sand eels are common, many bass anglers use these delicate little fish to the exclusion of all other bait and some magnificent catches of large bass have been taken on the natural eel. Unfortunately, sand eels die very quickly when confined in a bait can, but even a dead sand eel makes quite a good bait provided that it is fresh. The best way to collect a supply of sand eels is to use a special two-pronged fork (see Fig. 7). This is used to rake eels out of the damp sand at the water's edge. There is a knack to this, but once the technique has been mastered it becomes a simple operation to collect a plentiful supply of bait-sized sand eels. There are several ways of attaching a live sand eel to a hook, the best being to pass the hook point and barb through the lower jaw of the eel (see Fig. 8).

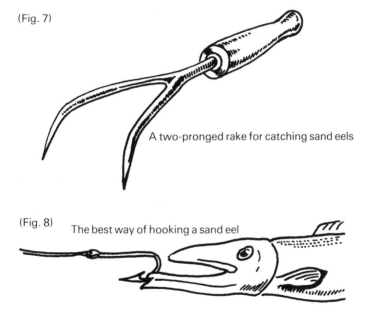

(Fig. 7)

A two-pronged rake for catching sand eels

(Fig. 8)   The best way of hooking a sand eel

Another effective method is to pass the hook through the flesh directly behind the head of the bait (see Fig. 9). A disadvantage of this method is that baits hooked in this way die quickly. Sand eels are fragile fish which seldom stand up to the shock of being cast any distance. The correct way of casting sand-eel baited float-tackle is to swing it out gently, so that the bait drops as softly as possible into the water.

Bass usually bite boldly on float tackle and consequently are fairly easy to hook. Largish hooks, however, are an advantage and hook size 2 or 1 freshwater scale is ideal.

(Fig. 9)

Sand eel hooked through
the back of its head

Using float-fished livebaits

Bass are fast-moving active hunters and in rocky areas they eat large numbers of immature wrasse, pouting, rockling, etc. Because of this, if you have no objections to the method, livebaiting can be most useful, although few anglers seem to realise the potential of this technique. The best way of presenting a small livebait is on float tackle, as this supports the bait well above the sea bed and prevents it from taking refuge among the rocks or weeds and so snagging the tackle.

A live fish bait is far heavier than a prawn or sand eel, and to support the extra weight a substantial float is necessary. The float I find most useful is a large-diameter pike pilot-float. These can be improved by inserting a short length of plastic tube through the centre hole bored in the float (see Fig. 10). This will stop the reel line from cutting into the cork body of the float when the strike is made. A float of this type slides freely, supports a large bait and offers little resistance to a taking fish. Pouting make first-class bass baits but small wrasse and rockfish collected from tide pools at low water are almost as good.

(Fig. 10)

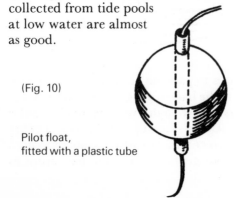

Pilot float,
fitted with a plastic tube

When livebaiting, a single size 4 or 6 treble hook gives more hooking power than a larger single hook and is thus preferable (see Fig. 11). Once a bass has taken a livebait it must be given time to get the bait well into its mouth; a premature strike will only pull the livebait away from the fish. The correct procedure is to give the bass line until enough time has elapsed for the fish to have turned the bait and started to swallow it.

(Fig. 11)

Livebait should be hooked on a size 4 or 6 treble hook

Bottom fishing

As bass of all sizes will browse over the sea bed in search of food, bottom fishing can be a most productive pastime. The only time bottom fishing from rocks is practical is when the rocks are surrounded by a clean sand or gravel bottom. Clean-bottomed gullies are also likely places, but for true bottom fishing it is advisable to select a rocky outcrop which projects into a sandy bay or beach.

A one-hook or two-hook running leger (see Fig. 12) is suitable for this type of fishing, although a single-boom paternoster (see Fig. 13) can also be used. Whenever possible, an extra-long trace should be used, as a bait which moves about over a wide area will be more attractive than a bait which is presented on a short trace. Bottom-fishing tackle often accounts for those extra-large bass which so many shore anglers dream about.

The 'big-baits-for-big-fish' idea certainly works where bass are concerned. There are, of course, exceptions to this rule but a large bait normally produces a fish of a higher-than-normal size. Whole fish, squidheads and kipper fillets all work very well. Despite the fact that it has been cured, kipper fillet is extremely good as it still contains a great deal of oil and, as bass seem to like smelly bait, a kipper often produces bites when fresh baits fail. Small squid used whole are first-class baits, as are small dead wrasse or pouting.

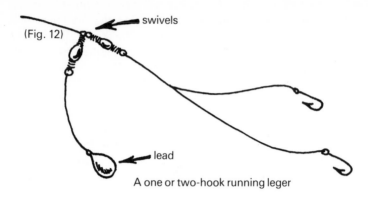

A one or two-hook running leger

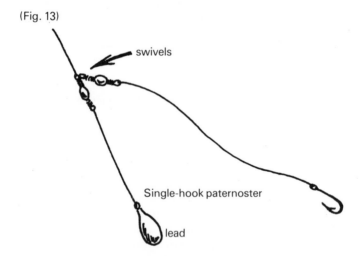

Single-hook paternoster

If you do not mind losing terminal tackle to snags, some good bass can be caught by fishing directly over rough ground. This can be a costly operation but losses can be cut by using old spark plugs in place of lead weights (tie a swivel to the spark plug with old line and tie your line to the other end of the swivel). These rough-ground bass are particularly fond of peeler crab or soft-shelled crab. These baits appear natural to the fish.

Bass fishing is both exciting and fascinating and many anglers specialise in this one species. The shore angler can easily specialise in this way, for bass of all sizes visit shore marks regularly and offer fine sport to the angler who is prepared to work hard for his fish.

It is advisable, when fishing coves and bays, to take careful notice of any natural features which are likely to attract bass. A small, inflowing stream of fresh water often interests bass, as fresh water attracts elvers and sand eels, both of which are prey to bass. A single rock, projecting above the sand, is another good bass-holding spot and a bait cast to fall close to an outcrop of this kind will usually catch more fish than a bait cast into a flat stretch of sand. The reason is obvious, bass gather near small projecting rocks, for the action of the tide dislodges all sorts of edible creatures which the waiting bass are quick to snap up. Peeler crabs or sand eels are a good bait under those conditions, for both are natural and both are likely to be found sheltering under or close to the rock. Bass are often bold biters and some anglers are content to jam their rods into a suitable crevice or into a rodstand and then sit back to wait for the bass to hook itself. This is lazy angling and not to be recommended, as many good bites will be missed. Personally I do not like to use a rod-rest of any description while bass fishing. I find that, by holding my rod at all times, I catch far more bass than would the lazy angler and miss few reasonable bites on the strike. My usual technique is to hold the rod so that the line between rod tip and bait is taut; at the first suggestion of a bite, I drop the rod tip slightly so that the fish is free to take a little line, then I strike at the next indication of a bite. Far too many anglers make a hash of striking by becoming over-excited. Self discipline is essential and should be learned at an early stage. Once you can control your initial reactions, striking becomes automatic. Far too many anglers snatch wildly at the rod at the first sign of a bite. This catches few fish, and bass are generally cautious feeders.

Methods (Boat)

Spinning

Spinning from a boat is similar to spinning from the shore. The same baits, tackle and tactics apply. The beauty of spinning for bass is that the fish are usually hooked in the lips and can be unhooked with miminal damage. With a natural bait the fish have a tendency to swallow both bait and hook, and often end

23

up hooked in the back of the throat. Under these circumstances it is impossible to remove the hook without damaging the delicate gill structure.

Trolling

Many anglers condemn trolling on the grounds that it is practically a commercial method of taking bass. I do not agree although I do admit that a trolled bait can be extremely deadly when bass are shoaling. Nine times out of ten, whenever a really huge catch of bass is reported in the angling press, the fish have fallen to baits trolled slowly behind a motor boat. Trolled baits must be fished behind a fairly substantial weight, otherwise the speed of the boat will cause the bait to kite up to the surface and drag along without working properly; unfortunately, to get the best sport out of trolling, the weight used should be kept to a minimum. To try to overcome this contradiction and the problem of additional weight, I have experimented with wire line for this form of fishing. Wire line is, in many ways, ideal for trolling. It has no elasticity, it has built-in weight and it allows the angler to keep in touch with the trailing bait. This is important. Contrary to popular belief, bass do not automatically hook themselves on a trolled bait. Use a nylon line which stretches on impact and you will lose a high percentage of the fish that bite. Wire line will hook far more fish but, and this is important, you still have to strike to set the hook. The lazy angler who is not prepared to hold his rod deserves what he gets, which is usually very little. Trolling like all forms of angling requires concentration. The moment a fish snaps at the lure you must strike back.

It is unwise to attach terminal tackle to the wire itself. For trolling purposes, I tie the bait to a 6 ft (1.8 m) length of 18 lb (8.2 kg) breaking-strain nylon. This is attached to the wire by means of a small stainless spiral link and single barrel swivel (see Fig. 14). With this sort of rig it is possible to fish with only a few ounces of lead, sufficient to hold the bait well beneath the surface where bass can see and intercept it. A banana-shaped lead (see Fig. 15) is the only lead that is streamlined enough for this. A roller tip-ring is, of course, essential for use with a wire line, no matter how thin or supple the line might be. You can troll with nylon or dacron lines. Of the two dacron, which does not stretch, is the best. Unfortunately dacron is slightly more buoyant and usually requires additional lead to hold down the bait.

(Fig. 14)

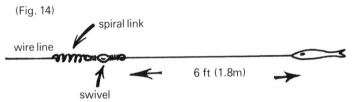

A spiral link and a swivel should be used to attach a trace to the wire line

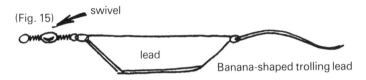

Banana-shaped trolling lead

Trolling calls for continual experiment. It is impossible to predict how far behind a boat the bass will feed on any given day. I have known bass pick up a bait almost as soon as it has been lowered into the water. On other occasions I have had a strike only when the bait trailed 50-60 yards (45-55 m) astern of the boat. Some days, of course, the bass shoal thickly on or just under the surface; other days they feed deep down. Because of this the angler who decides to troll must experiment with weights, rigs and distances to ascertain what the fish are doing at that time. Feeding patterns may change several times during a single day. When one productive combination fails, the angler must adapt his tackle until the fresh feeding level is discovered. The same applies to speed of retrieve. There are some days when the bass will only show interest in a fast-moving bait and others when they are feeling sluggish and will only strike at a bait fished slowly behind a boat whose engine is just, and only just, ticking over.

Bottom fishing

True bottom fishing, from an anchored or drifting boat has never been a popular method of bass fishing. Probably because most successful bass anglers are, by nature, restless and like to keep themselves and their baits on the move. Personally, I like to fish both ways and having had some good bass while bottom

25

fishing, I regard this style of angling as a worthwhile occupation. I do quite a lot of bottom fishing for big bass off the Hampshire coast in the Hurst Castle and Alum Bay areas of the Solent. Although I have yet to take a double-figure bass from either of these marks, both have produced very big specimens to bottom fishermen. The largest bass I can trace from Alum Bay weighed 16 lb (7.2 kg) and was taken on a legered livebait. The best taken at Hurst was 13 lb (5.9 kg) which fell to a legered squid bait. In the West Country estuaries bottom fishing is also practised by boat anglers, particularly on the Fowey river in south Cornwall.

For basic bottom fishing (using whole dead fish, squid or crab bait), it is advisable to use a plain running leger with a hook trace of no more than 4 ft (1.2 m) in length. Heavy rods, reels and lines should not be used for this work. Despite their obvious speed and power, bass are often shy-biting fish which pick up a bait very gently and give only a tiny bite indication in the process. With heavy tackle, this sort of bite may well go completely undetected. With light, sensitive tackle, the rod tip will give a clear indication of a bite, no matter how cautiously the fish takes the bait. I have caught a number of fine bass while bottom fishing in this way and although I have taken fish on squid and fish baits, peeler or soft crabs have always produced the most bites per session. Peeler or soft crabs are almost impossible to buy from bait dealers and most anglers make a point of collecting their own supply the day before they fish. Crabs change their shell once or twice a year, and it is during the first part of this process – when the old shell splits down the middle – that the crab becomes a *peeler*. Later, when it has entirely shed its old cracked shell and is busily engaged in growing a new one, it is known as a *softie* or *paper-backed* crab. The crab is obviously very vulnerable during the moulting stage and to avoid danger it takes refuge in any suitable retreat it can find. Once it has located a hiding place it will remain there until its new shell has hardened.

Moulting crabs are much sought after for bait and many anglers construct special traps to catch moulting crabs in quantity. These traps are so designed that the moulting crab, when searching for a safe retreat, will be tempted to crawl into the trap and stay there until the bait collector returns to empty them. Sections of old piping make good crab traps. These should be placed among weed-covered rock, well below the high-tide line. The angler who does not wish to use traps of this kind can usually collect bait crabs by turning over piles of thick weed close to projecting rocks, where moulting crabs usually collect.

Baiting up with soft and peeler crabs depends on the size of the crab itself. Small and medium ones can be used with the claws removed; or they can be used whole and alive. This is the best way, in my opinion. To use a paper-backed crab and keep it alive, the hook (point and bend) should be passed through the channel behind the crab's eyes (see Fig. 16). Very large peeler crabs can be used whole or cut in half. Without their shells these baits are very soft and it pays to tie them to the hook with a length of soft wool. Crabs in all stages of development can be kept alive for several days in a bucket containing a little sea water and a lot of fresh damp seaweed. Where possible, a container full of crabs should be kept in a cool dark place.

(Fig. 16)

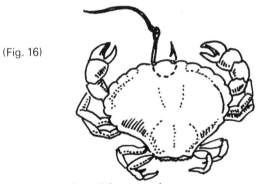

Crab hooked through its eye sockets

Bass are very adept at sucking crab off the hook, so hold the rod at all times and strike at the slightest indication of a bite. Squid and fish baits are much tougher, and bass tend to take these in a different way. So when squid or a fish bait is used, the rod can either be held or laid down according to preference.

Fishing with livebaits

Despite the fact that bass are known predators, few bass anglers bother to use any livebait other than sand eel. I have never understood why. A small wrasse or pouting makes a first class bass bait. Live sand eels have long been regarded as a top bass bait. In the West Country, where sand eels are common,

27

charter-boat skippers and anglers make a habit of catching a plentiful supply whenever a serious bass fishing expedition is planned. To catch sand eels in large quantities, a properly constructed fine-meshed seine net should be used. For gathering a few dozen eels, a sand-eel rake can be used. Using this calls for practice but once the technique has been mastered it is a simple-enough job to procure ample eels for a day's fishing. Sand eels come inshore to avoid predators and bury themselves in loose sand at the sea's edge. By pulling a rake firmly through the sand in the shallows, eels can be flipped out and caught with your free hand. Keeping them alive is far more difficult than catching them. In the long run the only container worth using is a specially constructed courge (wooden bait box – see Fig. 17), which has perforated sides. Captured eels should be placed in this as quickly as possible, and the box should be allowed to float at all times so that fresh sea water filters continuously through the perforations and keeps the eels alive. Sand eels are extremely delicate and at the slightest trace of rough handling or if the water becomes stale, they turn belly up and die. Handle them as little as possible and always make absolutely certain that the bait box is well perforated and clean, as a dirty bait box will quickly destroy freshly-caught sand eels. Sand eels can also be kept in a bait bucket, provided that a small battery-operated aeration unit is used at all times. These useful little units are obtainable from most tackle shops, but carry spare batteries at all times as if the pump stops the eels will start to die within minutes.

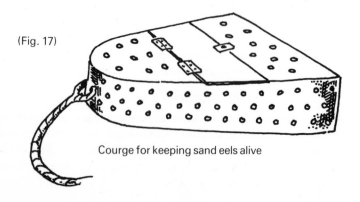

(Fig. 17)

Courge for keeping sand eels alive

Sand eels can be fished on a running leger, but they work best when allowed to swim as freely as possible. In Cornwall, where boat fishing for bass with live sand-eel baits has been brought to a fine art, the technique of long-link legering approaches perfection. Only very small leads are used and these are stopped 5 ft (1.5 m) from the hook. The method is to drop the bait into the water and pay out 20-40 ft (6-12.2 m) of line through the eye of the lead (see Fig. 18). Once the bait is well astern of the boat the lead is lowered to the bottom in the normal way, leaving the eel to range about naturally at the end of a very long tether.

(Fig. 18)

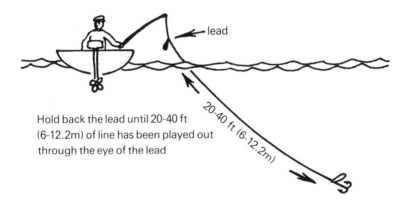

Hold back the lead until 20-40 ft (6-12.2m) of line has been played out through the eye of the lead

20-40 ft (6-12.2m)

Where the tidal current is fast, live eels should be hooked once through the lower part of the jaw (see Fig. 8). This allows the eel to move freely and breathe easily at all times. Some anglers prefer to pass the hook through the mouth, so that the point and barb project from the gill slit. This gives a firmer hook hold but makes it difficult for the eel to breathe. As already mentioned I find that sand eels hooked in this fashion expire very quickly. Under slack water conditions, the eel can be mounted by passing the hook through the flesh of the back, just behind the head. This gives a good hook hold but once again tends to kill the eel very quickly. Dead sand eels can, of course, be used but are far less effective than live eels where bass are concerned. Live sand eels are best fished over a flat-sand or mud bottom, where they would naturally live. Bass, hunting in these areas, expect to find sand eels present and take the bait with confidence. Small live fish of almost any type can be used on bottom tackle, but it is advisable to use a bait which conforms to the type of ground you are fishing over. For example, small wrasse, butterfish, blennies, etc, should always be fished over fairly rocky ground, for all these fish live on or close to rock and weed.

The size of hooks used for livebaiting depends entirely on the size of bait being used. Small sand eels, for example, should be used on size 1 or 2 hooks; larger eels on size 1-0 or 2-0. Live fish, which are much bulkier, are best fished on a size 4-0 fine-wire round-bend hook (see Fig. 19). Fish baits can be hooked through the lips or through the root of the tail. Float fishing from boats for bass is not widely done but it can be highly effective and is probably the best method of presenting a livebait yet devised. Choice of bait depends on the area to be fished, although practically any small rock fish can be used. Prawns or hermit crabs make extremely good float-fishing baits, and I have also had some good sport while using elvers (young silver eels) on float tackle.

(Fig. 19)

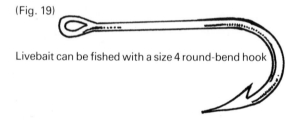

Livebait can be fished with a size 4 round-bend hook

Elvers are fairly easy to catch in quantity. They are found in estuaries or close to trickles of fresh water. I normally catch mine by turning over weed-covered stones at low water. Silver eels are slippery creatures at the best of times – and elvers are no exception – so it takes time to develop the knack of grabbing them the moment they are seen. The technique is easily learned and calls for nothing more than a combination of sharp eyes and quick reflexes. The moment the elvers are exposed to light, they quickly make off in the direction of the nearest cover. Once caught, they can be kept alive in a bait box containing a lining of wet sand covered by a few handfuls of fresh seaweed.

I catch most of my bass on elvers of 6 in or more (c 15 cm) in length. The only practical way to hook a live elver is through

30

the muscle at the back of its head. The tackle should be dropped into the water the moment the hook is baited, as elvers exposed to the air tend to tie themselves into a knot and climb the hook trace; once in this position, they are adept at levering themselves off the hook and escaping. Once in the water, however, they stop this, straighten out and try to escape by swimming away from the boat. Bass of all sizes eat elvers and, if the angler has access to an area where elvers are plentiful, they are well worth trying as a bass bait.

Prawns are another excellent bait. Prawns are, however, very delicate creatures and great care should be taken to ensure that they remain alive and practically undamaged during the process of attaching them to the hook. This is best achieved by hooking the prawn once through its second tail segment (see Fig. 20). A prawn hooked in this way will stay alive for a considerable time and, if a longish trace is used between hook and lead, the prawn should be able to swim about in a natural manner.

(Fig. 20)

Prawn hooked through its second tail segment

Gathering prawns for bait can be an interesting occupation and there are several methods to use. In rock gullies or harbours, these active creatures can be taken in a hand net which should be worked round the submerged weed fringes that cling to the rock or stonework as it is among this weed that the prawns live and feed. A more effective method, particularly for prawning in deep water, is the 'drop net' technique. Most sea anglers construct their own drop-net from the alloy rim of a bicycle wheel and a section of fine-meshed cotton netting. The finished drop-net is furnished with metal crossbars and is attached to a length of buoyed rope, the bottom of the net being weighted with a lead. To attract prawns, a dead fish should be lashed to the crossbars (see Fig. 21). The net can then be lowered into deepish water close to rocks or weed-covered stonework where prawns are thought to exist. After the net has been submerged for 5 to

31

10 minutes it should be raised rapidly and smoothly to the surface, so that any prawns attracted by the fish bait become trapped in the bag of the net. Prawns are fast, active creatures and they will skip over the rim of the net at the slightest sign of a jerk on the net rope. Because of this it is absolutely essential to raise the net in a smooth sweep.

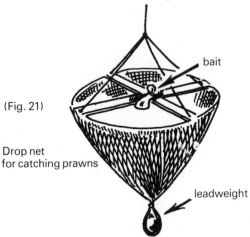

bait

(Fig. 21)

Drop net
for catching prawns

leadweight

For boat fishing purposes, prawns should be kept in a well-perforated tin container hung over the side of the boat. My own prawn tin is perforated at the top and sides only (see Fig. 22) so that, although sea water can circulate freely while the tin is immersed, the bottom half of the tin will still hold water when it is lifted out of the sea. In this way, prawns can be kept alive and in good condition while the boat is being moved from one mark to another. Dead prawns can be used to good effect on float tackle, particularly when the sea is choppy. The action of the waves causes the float to lift, which in turn activates the bait.

(Fig. 22)

Perforated tin
for keeping live prawns

32

Driftline fishing

Bass can be caught on driftline tackle which, as its name implies, is allowed to drift away from the boat with the tide. In overspill areas, or the mouth of a harbour where the water runs rapidly, a bait presented on a weightless or slightly leaded driftline can be killing. Driftline tackle is extremely simple; consisting of rod, reel, line, swivel and hook (the swivel is used to join the reel line to the hook trace). The hook trace should be 3-4 ft (0.9-1.2 m) long and have a breaking strain of no more than 6 lb (2.7 kg). Where there is strong tidal movement, a lead weight can be added to the tackle above the swivel (see Fig. 23). In slack water, however, it is often possible to fish without weights of any kind. Always bear in mind that the speed of the tide will change from hour to hour and constant adjustment of weight will be necessary to ensure that the terminal tackle continues to function properly. Large, soft split shot or half-moon leads of various sizes should be used as weights, as these can be added or subtracted as prevailing conditions change. Large baits, such as whole live fish of about 6 or 7 in (15 or 17.5 cm) are excellent for this sort of bass fishing.

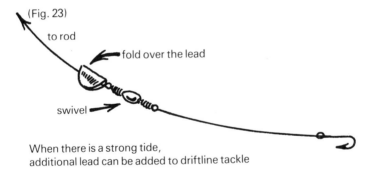

(Fig. 23)

to rod

fold over the lead

swivel

When there is a strong tide,
additional lead can be added to driftline tackle

On some of the offshore sandbanks along the south coast of England I have had excellent sport with bass by using whole king ragworms on weighted driftline tackle. The art is to place the boat so that the bait can be trundled over the lip of the sandbank into deeper water, where bass shoals wait to intercept any edible objects swept off the sandbanks by the action of the tide. This is a fascinating form of fishing. Invariably, bass hit the bait with a terrific bang, pulling the rod hard over with the power of their strike.

Black and Red Bream

Neither the red or black sea bream grows to any great size but both are game fighters on light tackle. Black bream, in particular, are very popular with boat anglers on the south coast of the British Isles. Unfortunately, both species appear to be rather limited in distribution, and northern anglers have little chance of catching either fish in their home areas. It is also rare for shore anglers to catch either of these fish.

The adult red bream is a handsome deep-bodied fish. Its dorsal fin is long, well shaped and spiny, and its beautiful pectoral fins are elongated and sickle shaped. A mature red bream is orange-red in colour with silvery-pink sides. To make identification even easier, it has a distinctive black patch on its shoulder close to the start of the lateral line; it also has very large eyes. An average rod-caught red bream weighs $1\frac{1}{2}$–$2\frac{1}{2}$ lb (0.75–1.1 kg) but weights up to almost 8 lb (3.6 kg) have been taken. Although I have taken many large red bream during the day in West Country waters while bottom fishing in deep water, red bream are nocturnal feeders which bite best after dark. Strangely enough, these fish (which are normally bottom feeders) often rise towards the surface during late evening. I have caught many bream while driftline fishing just under the surface. Small red bream live mainly on shellfish but the larger specimens eat almost anything that swims and is not too large. Although red bream are beautiful fish to look at they cannot compare in fighting spirit with black bream; which have an even more limited distribution. Although the odd black bream or two can be caught from any rough-ground mark in the English Channel, the main shoals are localised along one short section of the Sussex coast. Littlehampton is, without doubt, the best known

34

black-bream centre in Britain and most charter boats working from this port specialise in bream fishing during spring and early summer. But black bream have suffered badly from over fishing in recent years and, even at Littlehampton, immense catches are now rarely taken; although, at one time, it was common for a single boat to land several hundredweight of big bream each time it went out. In recent years, good catches of black bream have been made off the Isle of Wight and also off Poole and Weymouth in Dorset. On distant offshore marks from Sussex to Cornwall, most wreck marks produce big bream in quantity.

Black bream are similar in shape to red bream. The pectoral fins, however, are not as long and as its name implies, the black bream is a dusky fish. The basic body colour is dark bluish-grey and the underparts are silvery white. Black bream that live on really rough ground often have dark vertical bands down their sides. Although black bream never reach the size of red bream, fish of between 3-4 lb (1.4-1.8 kg) are common along the Sussex coasts. Even a medium-sized specimen will put up a magnificent fight on all but the heaviest of tackle. The diet of black bream is similar to that of red bream, and fish cuttings, worms and squid make the best baits. A mixture, such as squid and worm, is deadly. Combination baits of this kind often produce fish when conventional baits fail.

Like all south-coast boat anglers, I hope that new black bream hot-spots will be discovered during the next few seasons. It would be a great pity if such a fine fighting species were to become a rarity through anglers over fishing a particular area and killing too many stock fish in the process. Six bream, for example, are enough for any angler to take at one time: to finish a day with a sack of unwanted dead bream is unforgivable. I am hopeful that black bream will make a comeback. Red bream did this some years ago, at a time when everybody assumed that they were on the verge of extinction. Now they swarm in large numbers; with luck, and with care on the part of the angler, black bream will reappear in similar quantity.

Tackle

Sea bream are essentially a light-tackle fish. Unfortunately, many anglers still fish bream grounds with heavyweight gear, giving the fish little opportunity to show their fighting ability.

My advice to anglers who wish to enjoy their bream fishing is to use only the lightest tackle. My own choice is a light spinning rod and a tiny multiplier of the Abu 6500 type (or a favoured Grice and Young centre-pin reel), loaded with line of 7 or 8 lb (3.2 or 3.6) breaking strain. Even diminutive black bream in the 1½ lb (0.7 kg) class put up a battle on this sort of gear. Whereas, even a huge specimen hooked on a standard boat rod can be winched straight up to the boat.

Hook sizes for black or red bream should range from size 1 to 8 (freshwater scale). Both types of fish have small mouths and, with light tackle, a big hook would be difficult to set when the strike is made.

Sea bream should be brought into the boat with a medium sized landing net. This is simple to use and allows unwanted fish to be returned unharmed to the sea.

Methods

Black bream shoal and feed at different levels at varying stages of the tide. At slack water, for example, they usually feed on the bottom. But as the tide starts to run they rise towards the surface. Red bream, on the other hand, stay on the bottom during the day and only start to rise to the surface as night begins to fall. For both species a plain running leger is the best terminal rig to use. In the case of the black bream it should incorporate an extra-long flowing trace. As a rough guide, the length of the trace should equal the length of the rod. Leads should be kept as small as possible. On many occasions, while fishing with extra-fine lines, I have found I can touch the bottom quite easily with a ½–¾ oz (0.014–0.021 kg) weight. Obviously, the strength of the tidal run will dictate the amount of lead to be used, but with fine lines it is seldom necessary to use more than 2 or 3 oz (0.057 or 0.085 kg) on any of the known British bream grounds. The lead should be allowed to run freely on the line, being stopped only by a small swivel used to connect the line with the trace. For red bream, it is best to hold the bait in one position for as long as possible but for black bream a moving bait catches the most fish. I catch most of my black bream by letting down the tackle until the lead touches bottom, then retrieving it slowly until either a fish takes the bait or the tackle breaks surface. Both types of bream are bold biters, but the black bream is a real rod-tip rattler. It is advisable to ignore the first few tugs and wait until the fish actually pulls the rod over, and holds it over, before striking. The best baits for bream fishing are ragworm, lugworm, fish strips or mussels. Long strips of squid and whole small sand eels can also be used. At Littlehampton it was once common for black bream anglers to use cooked rice grains.

Paternoster

A light paternoster can be used to catch both species of bream. It should be made up with a 3 ft (0.9 m) trace. I find I get better results with the paternoster when I bump it up and down over the bottom by lifting the rod tip and letting out a few yards/metres of line at the same time. The paternoster works well astern of a boat, and bites will often occur when it is on the move.

Float fishing

I have had many large catches of red bream in West Country waters while float fishing in comparatively shallow water. The float I use, takes 1 to 1½ oz (0.028–0.042 kg) of lead, which is sufficient to hold the bait down during the slack part of the tide or during most stages of a full neap tide. Normally I set the tackle so that the lead is about 1 ft (0.3 m) off the bottom. The float is, of course, a slider which is stopped on the line by means of a piece of rubber band. To avoid the stop from becoming wedged in the centre tube of the float, it is advisable to run a small button on the line between float and rubber stop.

Bream bite extremely well on float tackle, and although you are likely to miss some bites while using this technique, the sight of a bright float disappearing abruptly from sight makes it a most enjoyable experience. Both species of bream fight well and on light tackle there can be no question of hauling them to the surface. Expert black-bream fishermen sometimes fish with freshwater trotting rods and 5 lb (2.3 kg) line. To control a big bream on tackle as light as this calls for considerable skill. I would not advise novice anglers to try their luck with this tackle, until they have caught a fair number of big sea bream on heavier tackle.

Black bream respond well to groundbait. Many charter-boat skippers who fish black bream marks, make a habit of attaching a fine mesh bag full of mashed up fish flesh to the anchor rope, just above the anchor chain, before dropping it over the side. In slack tides, further ground bait can be mixed into heavy solid balls and dropped over the side at regular intervals. A simple groundbait dispenser can be made from a 35 mm film can which has a series of holes punched in its side. This container can be filled with cotton wool soaked in fish oil and attached to the line directly above the weight.

Cod, Whiting, Haddock and Pouting

In the south of the British Isles, cod are the main quarry of winter fishermen. The first fish of the season generally put in an appearance during late September or early October.

Cod have always been common in the English Channel and in the North Sea, but ten years ago the shoals of cod extended their range further westward and are now commonly caught over West Country wreck marks.

In northern waters cod are a summer species occurring in large numbers during late June and July. The exception to this is the Gantocks area in the Firth of Clyde where huge cod catches sometimes occur during March. In the south, the Kent and Sussex coast often produce vast numbers of cod and codling, but it is the Needles area, off the Isle of Wight in Hampshire, that produces big cod in good numbers. The average size of the fish caught there is probably greater than anywhere else in the British Isles. Cod of 20 lb (9.1 kg) are commonplace off the island and the largest cod yet caught in this area tipped the scales at 44 lb 8 oz (20.2 kg). I have caught Isle of Wight cod to 38 lb (17.2 kg) and have seen a number of 40 lb (18.1 kg) specimens brought ashore. Isle of Wight cod are seldom numerous, but what they lack in numbers they make up for in weight. During the 1969 season I was fortunate enough to take part in the largest-ever recorded catch of cod around the Isle of Wight – 20 fish with the staggering total gross weight of 450 lb (204 kg). Only one fish weighed under 20 lb (9.1 kg) that day, and we boated six fish of over 30 lb (13.6 kg). Cod have always been sought after by boat anglers, but since the fish changed their habits and extended their range they have become the most popular winter sea fish on the British list. I expect the cod record to rise to 60 lb (27.2 kg) in the future, and commercial records show that cod can reach 100 lb (45.4 kg) or more. From the angler's point of view, cod have much to recommend them. Even a small cod is a largish fish and a big one is truly enormous; and cod of all sizes make excellent eating!

In times of economic depression cod makes a welcome addition to a family menu and a few good-sized cod, filleted and kept in a deep freeze, can amply repay tackle, bait and general fishing costs.

The cod is not a pretty fish. Its huge head, pot belly and tapering cylindrical body give it an ugly look. Even so, a big cod fresh from the sea and in the very pink of condition has an attraction all of its own. Cod do not rate very highly in terms of fighting ability, and although their bulk and obvious strength makes them difficult to pump up from any depth of water, they rarely show any spirit and are usually content to plug round right under the boat. Shore anglers probably get the best sport out of cod fishing. Particularly when big fish are hooked in heavy seas.

Feeding habits

Cod are bottom feeders. They tend to live in fairly deep water where they will eat practically anything that comes their way. I am amazed at the stomach contents of the cod I catch; this has included large stones, odd bits of metal and wire, bottle tops, paper, bones, white plastic cups, whole crabs, small lobsters and fish of many kinds. As far as natural food is concerned, anything that swims or crawls over the sea bed and is small enough to eat becomes fair game to the ever-hungry cod shoals.

Tackle

Boat rods

Almost any strong hollow-glass boat rod can be used to catch cod. For anglers wishing to take cod fishing seriously, I advise a more specialised rod. Unfortunately, most rod manufacturers still seem to believe that the maximum length of a boat rod should be 6½ ft (2 m), as this is the easiest length to handle in a boat. Although a rod of this length is serviceable, a good cod-fishing rod should be at least 6 in (15 cm) longer. There are a few rod builders who have recognised the need for longer rods, a notable example being the uptide casting rods being used for east-coast boat fishing. These rods measure 9 or 10 ft (2.7 or 3 m) and are used to cast a bait uptide, out from a boat. Their lengths are interesting but in my opinion their use is limited to that small east-coast area where localised conditions decree that techniques must be employed to keep the bait away from the boat. This is a 'do-it-yourself' age and good quality hollow-glass rod blanks can be purchased at a reasonable price. The home-handyman can, therefore, produce his own *super de luxe* boat rods at approximately half the cost of a shop-bought rod. When purchasing glass blanks, it is essential to give thought to what you will require; for the great advantage of building your own rod is that you can choose the fitting you personally desire. My own rod, for example, has a steep taper and a test curve of around 10 lb (4.5 kg). Which means that it will handle lines of from 25–50 lb (11.3–22.6 kg) breaking strain. The steep taper gives plenty of progressive power to the rod, yet the actual tip is thin enough to transmit the tiniest bite. The rod also has a roller-tip ring and heavy steel guide rings. The roller is vital, for it allows me to use nylon, braided or wire lines as I wish. A rod fitted with an ordinary tip ring would be useless for fishing with metal line, due to the constant line kinks, which a roller tip automatically straightens out as the tackle is being retrieved. A boat rod should be bought or designed to match the reel you intend to use. This is important. A badly-matched set of tackle can make angling difficult and unpleasant.

Beach rods

Choosing a beach rod is seldom easy. Rod styles tend to change from one area to the next. Your local tackle dealer can often point you in the right direction but if not, my advice is to purchase a 12 ft (3.6 m) rod capable of casting leads in the 6–8 oz (0.170–0.226 kg) range. This may sound like a heavy weapon but on good cod-fishing days, when rough seas bring the fish inshore, heavy leads may have to be used to keep the bait in place. Modern trends are moving towards rods capable of distance casting and anglers talk incessantly of casting 140 yards/metres plus: often overshooting the fish. Remember, long casting was developed to fish a specific area off Dungeness beach. Most anglers can produce fish at distances of 50 — 100 yards/

metres from the shore. Do not fall into the common trap of trying to outcast the tournament angler. Learn to long cast by all means, but temper your casting to suit the locality.

Reels

A medium-sized multiplier is ideal for cod fishing. When buying one of these reels for boat fishing, make sure that it is fitted with a metal or fibreglass spool that will not crack under stress, as nylon line in particular contracts under pressure and a reel with a plastic spool will soon become unserviceable when used against a heavy fish such as cod. My own reels for cod are a Mitchell 624 and a Tatler 2½-0 for use with wire line. Medium-sized multiplying reels are readily available, so make sure that the one you buy is backed by a fast and efficient aftersales service.

For beach casting you can use a multiplier or fixed-spool reel. As far as I am concerned the best multipliers are the Abu 7000C, the Penn Squidder and the Mitchell 602 AP. Fixed-spool reels are now coming into their own for shore fishing and many good patterns are available. For casting heavy leads, a fixed-spool reel with a simple finger pick-up is preferable to one with the full bale-arm system.

Lines

Nylon lines provide unbeatable value if you are worried about price. But for reliability, braided lines are best for boat fishing. A line of 30 or 35 lb (13.6 or 15.9 kg) breaking strain is ideal for general cod fishing although more experienced anglers often fish with lighter line in an attempt to get sport from the cod they catch. Cod are often caught in strong tides. As mentioned, to fish successfully in a heavy tide, the bait must be presented on or very close to the sea bed. To do this you must either fish with a nylon or braided line, which needs a very heavy lead to hold it down, or else with an all-metal line which, being thinner, creates less water resistance than other lines and, being heavier in itself, sinks by its own weight, enabling you to fish with very light leads. The only wire lines readily available are single-strand Monel metal and braided lines.

Many cod anglers buy metal line, use it once, and then discard it as useless or unmanageable. I know how they feel. Unless you use a rod fitted with a roller-tip ring that works, and make absolutely certain that you guide the wire back on to the reel spool with the ball of your thumb, metal line does tend to kink up and bunch on the reel. Some anglers use a leather thumbstall to protect their skin from the metal line. I have never found this to be essential, but it can save blisters if you intend to fish on two or three consecutive days. Bites registered on wire are much more definite than bites registered on any other kind of line, mainly because the wire enables you to keep in direct contact with the lead and bait. With nylon or braided line, a bow is almost inevitable (see **Fig. 24**). Consequently it is very difficult, if not practically impossible to remain in contact with the terminal tackle except at dead-slack water.

(Fig. 24)

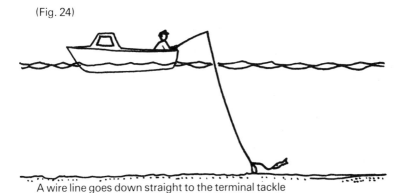

A wire line goes down straight to the terminal tackle

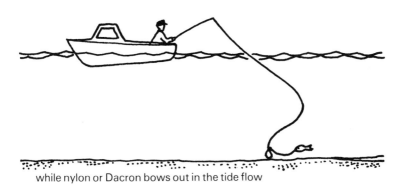

while nylon or Dacron bows out in the tide flow

43

Of the two main types of wire, I prefer the Monel metal variety. It is thicker than braided wire of a similar breaking strain, and it doesn't fray in the same way. I have lost more good fish than I care to remember on braided wire, so now I stick to single-strand Monel lines.

Nylon lines should always be used for cod fishing from the shore. Nylon is cheap, tough, easy to cast and no other type of line is so adaptive. Expert cod anglers fish with lines of 14 or 16 lb (6.3 or 7.2 kg) breaking strain. Novices, however, should use lines of 20 or even 25 lb (9.1 or 11.3 kg) breaking strain. Once experienced, they can then use lighter tackle. North Country cod anglers, who normally fish over excessively rough grounds, regularly use lines of 30 lb (13.6 kg) breaking strain to combat the abrasive action of the rocks.

Hooks and terminal tackle

Cod have huge mouths. A 15 lb (6.8 kg) cod can swallow a 3 lb (1.4 kg) whiting with no trouble at all. Because of this, I consider big hooks to be absolutely essential for cod fishing from boats. Even a bunch of lugworm should be presented on a size 4-0, and larger baits – such as squid or fish fillets – requires 6-0 or 8-0 hooks to hold them in place. Shore anglers should use 4-0 hooks.

The cod is a heavy fish which often lives in deep water and fast tides; it is advisable to take this into account and select your hooks with an eye to their strength as well as their size. My own favourite is a flat-forged bronzed hook manufactured by Mustad Ltd. Remember, however, that sharp hooks cannot be bought in tackle shops, so each hook you buy should be carefully sharpened. Cod hooks should be razor sharp; the inside of a cod's mouth is bony, and a blunt hook will lose you fish after fish. I make a point of touching up the point of my hook after catching a fish.

Cod can be caught on a plain nylon trace but it helps to use a trace made up of a length of nylon-covered wire which has the same breaking strain as the reel line. I advocate the use of wire because a big cod has a number of pads of short sharp teeth in its mouth and its gill rakers are also armed.

Cod traces of nylon-covered wire should be made up in 2 ft (0.6 m) lengths, with a swivel at one end and the hook at the other (see Fig. 25).

44

(Fig. 25)

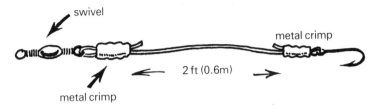

swivel

metal crimp

metal crimp

2 ft (0.6m)

Cod trace of nylon-covered wire

Methods

Cod are a bottom-dwelling species, which means that whatever method is used, the bait must be presented on or very close to the seabed. For fishing in areas where cod are numerous and of a fairly low average size, a two-hook or three-hook paternoster trot (see Fig. 26) is probably the most killing method to use. The paternoster trot is designed to catch codling and is therefore best used with smallish baits, such as bunched lug or ragworms, fish, squid strips and shellfish. When fishing a mark where large cod are known to exist, it is best to use a single-hook leger as multi-hook tackle may well attract two or more big fish at the same time, and they will inevitably smash the line once they feel the pressure of the rod tip.

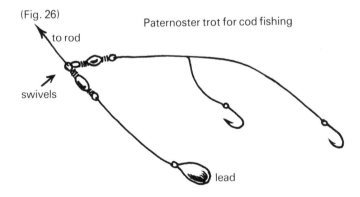

(Fig. 26)   Paternoster trot for cod fishing

to rod

swivels

lead

Cod were once regarded as slow and stupid fish, which could be lugged out on any rubbishy terminal tackle. This viewpoint was probably the main reason why a 32 lb (14.5 kg) cod held

the cod record for over 30 years. Modern anglers, however, discovered that by putting considerable thought into cod fishing,
it was possible to catch dozens of fish over the weight of the old
record specimen. At present nine out of every ten big cod are
taken on a single-hook running leger. The real secret of catching big cod is the ability to judge accurately the length of trace
to use on a given day. This length varies considerably. Only
continual practice and experience can tell you just what to use
each time you go out. As a basis, however, I would advise the
newcomer to start by leaving a distance of 5 ft (1.5 m) between
lead and hook (see Fig. 27). The lead should be clipped directly
to a plain Kilmore link, which should be threaded onto the line
with a single large plastic bead at either side of it, so that it can
slide freely at all times. The beads will stop the Kilmore link
from jamming. The shape of the lead depends on whether you
want the baited tackle to stay in one place or to roll slowly over
the sea bed. For static work a flat or pyramid-shaped lead
should be used but, when rolling the bait out, a bomb-shaped
lead is better. The majority of the cod I catch are taken well
astern of the boat on rolling-leger tackle.

(Fig. 27)

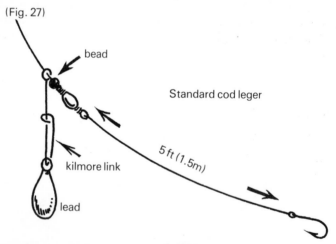

bead

Standard cod leger

kilmore link

5 ft (1.5m)

lead

When a wire line is used for this rolling-leger technique, it is
essential to use a nylon leader on which the leger can run. A
weight attached to the actual wire will jam up in use, due to
kinking in the wire. This does not occur when a nylon leader is
used (see Fig. 28). The leader should be at least 6 ft (1.8 m) in

length and should be joined to the wire reel-line by a strong swivel. Never tie the nylon directly to the wire, or a break will be inevitable.

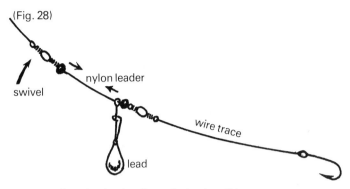

(Fig. 28)

swivel

nylon leader

wire trace

lead

The use of a nylon leader allows the lead to slide

The rolling-leger method is simple to use. First, the tackle is sent down to the bottom, as close under the boat as possible. Second, by lifting the rod tip and, at the same time, releasing the reel spool (so that 2-3 yards/metres of line run out) the lead is bounced along the sea bed, away from the boat. This process is repeated at regular intervals and the tackle worked steadily over the bottom. It is possible, with wire line, which allows you to remain in direct contact with the terminal tackle, to work the bait out for about 150 yards/metres and still be able to detect bites.

This form of angling calls for absolute concentration. It is impossible to rest the rod and still fish the rolling leger properly: to be successful the rod must be held all the time that the bait is in the water. The static leger is a less exacting style of angling, well suited to anglers who do not want to work too hard for their fish. A comparison of catches, however, will soon show the rolling leger to be consistently the most successful technique. The shore angler will catch most fish using a simplified paternoster trot rig (see Fig. 29). This will cast well and present the bait at the right depth. Some anglers use a two-hook or even three-hook rig. I prefer a single hook: as mentioned, two or more cod hooked in rough seas can easily break a line, while the fish can usually be beached without fear of breakage.

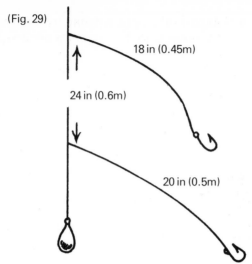

(Fig. 29)

18 in (0.45m)

24 in (0.6m)

20 in (0.5m)

Paternoster rig for cod fishing from the shore

Probably the finest cod bait available to the boat angler is small white Californian squid. This is imported in vast quantity and sold in 5 lb (2.3 kg) packs. A pack should be enough to keep three anglers in bait for a whole day's cod fishing. These squid, which average 6-7 in (15-17.5 cm) in length, can be used whole or cut up. I find that by breaking off the head section and cutting the end of the body mantle into strips to move with the tide flow I hook more cod than if I use the squid whole.

The main attraction of the squid for cod is probably its whiteness, which must show up well in the water. To add to the attractiveness of the bait, I often use it in conjunction with two dead sprats hooked once through their eye sockets. The sprats hang on either side of the squid and act as flashers, attracting the attention of a prowling cod shoal.

On some occasions, when the fish are slow to bite, an attractor-spoon can be added to the trace (see Fig. 30). The best spoon for this work is a 3 in (7.5 cm) white plastic spoon, which will flash well as it moves with the tide but will not twist the trace by revolving. I have had many good cod on this leger/spoon combination. Beach anglers tend to use worm baits in preference to squid. Obviously, in shallower water cod see worms as a natural item of food. Down at Dungeness, and on the east-coast cod beaches, bunched lugworm is *the* bait. Personally, I feel that a hungry cod will snatch at just about anything it comes across. Even so, when worm works, why try other baits?

(Fig. 30)

plastic spoon

6-12 in
(0.15-0.3m)

A plastic attractor-spoon attached to a cod trace

Artificial baits

Cod are confirmed predators, and fishermen in many parts of the world make their living by jigging for cod with shiny lead lures covered in sharp hooks. In commercial fishing circles these baits are known as *Rippers*, a very apt name, for half of the fish caught in this way are foul-hooked. As most anglers are not interested in catching cod in quantity by foul means, an acceptable version of the commercial ripper has been produced for everyday cod fishing.

Scandinavian fishermen have brought the use of artificial lures for cod to a fine art and regard them as the premier cod bait. British anglers have not yet reached this stage but I feel it won't be long before they do, and artificial lures become the accepted bait in Britain for cod fishing.

Most of the cod jigs available come from Scandinavia, and the best known are the famous pirk baits (see Fig. 31), produced by Abu of Sweden. At present, baits up to 1½ lb (o.7 kg) can be obtained. Pirk baits are usually tied directly to the end of the reel line, although I find that they work best when attached to a wire line, as the weight of the line tends to hold them close to the bottom irrespective of the state of the tide. Pirk baits are worked on the jigging principle (by raising and lowering the rod tip, so that the bait continually rises from the sea bed and then drops back with a fluttering motion).

(Fig. 31)

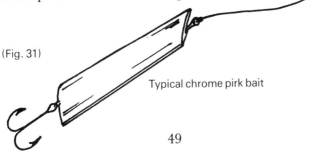

Typical chrome pirk bait

49

Shop-bought pirks are fitted with large-sized treble hooks. I prefer to remove these, substituting a 8-o single hook, as I find that the treble hook tends to foul-hook far too many fish, whereas most of the fish I take on bait fitted with a single hook, are caught fair and square inside the mouth.

Pirks can be used as they are, or they can be baited. I have caught fish with both, but for consistent catches a baited pirk is best. Small lures are probably best in areas where codling are plentiful; but when very big cod are known to exist in an area, my advice is to use the largest pirk bait you can buy.

Cod take pirk bait savagely, often hooking themselves firmly in the process. They also put up a better fight than fish hooked on leger or paternoster trot tackle, probably because they do not have to fight the weight of the lead as well as the constantly-applied rod pressure.

Artificial jigging-lures of the pirk-type are easy to construct at home, and the average angler should have no trouble in designing his own at a fraction of the price of the shop-bought varieties.

Cod feathers

Cod feathers are an enlarged version of standard mackerel feathers – although cod seem to prefer a lure made out of plain-white hackle feathers – whereas mackerel prefer bright colours. Cod feathers can be made at home by lashing a bunch of long white turkey hackles to a size 6-o hook. To ensure that the lashing does not unravel during use, it is advisable to thoroughly cover the thread with two coats of a fast-drying adhesive compound. A string of cod feathers should contain only two or three lures, as it is quite possible to hook more than one fish at a time when cod are shoaling thickly and a string of more than three feathers can lead to disaster. I only feather for cod when fishing areas noted for fish of medium size, as two or three codling hooked at one time can provide first class sport on ordinary boat tackle: on big-fish ground, I dispense entirely with feathers or else fish with just one. In this way I can be certain of being able to handle any fish that takes the lure.

Cod and tide change

It is still a general belief among anglers in Britain that the optimum time for cod fishing is at the top or bottom of the tide;

in other words, during the slack or dead-water period. This is a fallacy, created by the fact that many anglers found it difficult to fish when the tide was on the move: the only time they could fish properly being the change-over period, when their tackle was straight up and down over the side of the boat. I do not doubt for a moment that some cod can be taken during dead water, but carefully-kept records of catches taken during the past ten cod seasons have shown that four out of every five cod caught were taken during the time when the tide was running up or down. Slack-water fish are, in fact, fairly rare catches and sport often drops off as the dead-water period approaches. As soon as the tide begins to turn, the fish come on feed, and, as a rule, can be caught steadily throughout the ebb or flood tide. This applies to hard spring tides as well as to slack neap tides.

I am afraid that British anglers are still too tied to tradition for their own good; laziness being, of course, the main problem. Rather than try to fish properly in a hard tide, far too many people are content to leave the rod to fish for itself, propped up over the stern of the boat. An unattended rod seldom catches fish, mainly because, unless the angler is prepared to release a few yards/metres of line every few minutes, the pressure of water on a tight line will soon lift the lead and bait off the sea bed and cause it to kite up and hang well above the bottom. It does not catch fish in this condition; all it does is further the nonsensical belief that cod and other species are seldom caught before or after the slack-water period. The angler who is prepared to apply some thought will soon find that the fish are there to catch, provided that he or she is willing to work for them. The same applies to beach angling. The angler who tries, catches fish; while the lazy angler seldom goes home with good fish.

Whiting

If whiting grew to the size of cod they would be a marvellously sporting fish to catch on rod and line, for their streamlined body and rather pointed head give them a much greater turn of speed than cod. Unfortunately, the average whiting caught in British waters weighs between $1\frac{1}{2}$-2 lb (0.7-0.9 kg). Fish of double this weight can be regarded as large specimens, and the largest whiting I have taken weighed exactly $4\frac{1}{2}$ lb (2.04 kg).

One look at the tooth-filled mouth of the whiting reveals it as a true predator; which lives by preying on small fish.

Whiting have a very wide distribution and can be caught almost anywhere from one end of the British Isles to the other. This, coupled with their obvious value as a table fish, makes them popular with the average sea angler who likes to return home with a catch that people can eat and enjoy.

Like cod, whiting are a winter species, although boat anglers who fish deep marks that are well offshore often catch large bags of good-sized whiting during the summer and autumn months. Although small live fish form the basic diet of whiting, they often resort to bottom feeding as well. Because of this, they can be caught on almost any natural bait. Large whiting can be caught if you are prepared to fish for them. The real secret is using the right bait. I find that the majority of the large whiting I catch, fall to sprat baits. Long strips of squid, cut to resemble a sand eel also produce good results, as does fish-strip bait.

Generally speaking, whiting feed just off the sea bed, so a light two-hook or three-hook paternoster rig is probably the best terminal tackle to use for boat fishing. A light running-leger, with a long trace between lead and hook can also be useful, particularly when the tide is running too fast to use a paternoster properly. Unlike cod, whiting often go 'on feed' during the slack-water period and, when whiting have been scarce, this is often the period that saves the day. Whiting should be fished for with as light a set of tackle as possible. For boat fishing, light spinning rods or 12 lb (5.4 kg) class boat rods are ideal. Whiting will come well to artificial lures and a string of baited mackerel feathers will often produce good catches. I have also caught whiting on small (baited and unbaited) pirk baits.

Haddock

Few anglers have the chance to indulge in serious haddock fishing. For although these fish once had a widespread distribution, they have become rare, due to being over-fished by commercial boats. There are, however, signs that haddock may make a comeback. Numerous haddock were taken in the Thames Estuary and as far south as Hayling Island during the 1980 season. To catch haddock in any quantity, it is necessary to fish from the west coast of Scotland. I have caught haddock to 6 lb (2.7 kg) from marks around the Isle of Mull. The largest haddock, however, come from Cornish marks where specimens over 10 lb (4.5 kg) are often encountered. Haddock of truly record-breaking proportions exist on the 'Field', a mark directly out from the Dodman Point several miles south of the fishing village of Mevagissey in Cornwall, and average specimens weigh over 7 lb (3.2 kg). Some of the fastest haddock fishing I have ever encountered was in Northern Ireland. Haddock are common off the Antrim coast, and the Causeway Bank area, off Port Rush, produced fantastic catches. Not big fish – just a constant stream of average specimens.

Haddock are closely related to cod and there is a strong resemblance between the two species. The haddock, however, can be identified by a slightly-forked tail, black lateral line and dark spot on either side of its body. Haddock are exclusively bottom feeders and, although they will eat small fish if they can catch them, their main food consists of marine worms, crustacea, starfish and various molluscs. Whiting tackle is best for haddock fishing, and most of the fish I have caught have been taken on fish or squid-strip bait. At first a large haddock on lightish tackle puts up a fair fight but, like cod, it soon gives up.

Pouting

Anglers who specialise in salt-water competition fishing are the only people who like pouting. To them, the easily-caught pouting is a godsend. At most of the 'weigh ins' I have witnessed, pout have been the main fish brought to the scales and the average angler regards pout as a bait-robbing nuisance; even pouting of specimen-size usually fail to arouse much enthusiasm!

In appearance, the pouting is an attractive deep bodied fish, copper in colour, with or without dark vertical stripes, depending on whether the fish lives on rocky or sandy ground. Pouting will take almost any bait and can be caught on any type of bottom-fishing tackle. Even very big pouting put up little resistance when hooked, though small pouting make first class bass, tope, skate and conger baits. They must, however, be used fresh. Indeed, one local name for pouting is 'stink alive', which suits it well, for once caught pouting quickly start to decompose.

Conger

The conger record, which stood at 84 lb (38 kg) for over 40 years, has been smashed so many times by West Country wreck fishermen that I doubt if anyone can say accurately just how many 85 lb (38.5 kg) or over eels have been taken since wreck fishing became a serious sport. The record is held at present by a 109 lb 6 oz (49.6 kg) eel caught from a wreck mark, south-east of the Eddystone Lighthouse. A number of other 100 lb (45.3 kg) plus specimens have also been recorded.

All these fish came as a direct result of boatmen making intensive and constructive attacks on the huge eels known to inhabit the wrecks off the south and south-west coastline of Britain. No doubt another record-breaker will be taken from a similar mark during the next few years, with a fish up to 120 lb (54.3 kg) or more being a distinct possibility. Wrecks provide these giant eels with an ideal habitat; plenty of cover, and ample supplies of fish, being always available to the lurking eels. Unfortunately, many monster conger have been hooked and lost in the jumbled ironwork of rusting wrecks, and I believe that luck plays a bigger part in breaking the conger record than in any other type of angling. If you have the luck to hook a big conger outside of its retreat, and if you have the luck to lift it up and away from its home in the first few seconds of the battle, then you stand a fair chance of bringing it to the gaff.

Hooking conger is not a problem, boating them is. Skill plays little part in the actual playing of a really large conger. An absolute novice, with luck on his side, is just as likely to break the record if he can muster the initial brute force needed to pump the eel up from the sea bed. Experience can, of course, be a great help but is in no way essential. Nevertheless, it would be stupid to believe that all large congers are caught in this fashion, and the vast majority of anglers who boat large catches of conger are very experienced indeed. No one can really say just what weight a conger can reach. There is even evidence to show that 200 lb (90.6 kg) specimens are probable, although I doubt whether a fish of this calibre could be successfully caught on rod and line: a specimen of 250 lb (113.2 kg) was caught in a trawl by a Belgian fishing boat of the Westmann Isles. Basically a timid creature, which retreats at the slightest sign of danger, a big conger is the most-powerful fish any sea angler can expect to encounter off the British coast. The power of a fighting conger is prodigious, and it takes a strong and fit person to deal with a really large specimen. Very big conger are regarded as an offshore species by most sea anglers, and deep-water wrecks are where most big congers are caught. The odd thing, however, is that records show that the majority of the very large eels recorded were found washed up in estuaries or on beaches. In several cases, the fish were still alive when found and, in all the instances I have traced, those that were dead were in a reasonably fresh condition. Indicating, to my mind, that they had all been living comparatively close to the shore; not well out to sea as most anglers suppose. For example, a monster eel weighing 180 lb (81.5 kg) was washed ashore on the French coast in 1961, another, of 142 lb (64.3 kg), turned up on Walcott Beach, Norfolk in 1956 and another, weighing 96 lb (43.5 kg), was found barely alive at Minehead in Somerset in 1959. Two other giant specimens have also been found, one, of 90 lb (40.7 kg), was washed up at Portland in Dorset in 1956 and one, weighing 86 lb (38.9 kg), washed up in the Orwell Estuary, Suffolk, in 1961. Finally, an eel weighing 84 lb (38 kg) was washed ashore on the north Yorkshire coast in 1957 and an 87 lb (39.4 kg) specimen was caught by hand on the North Wales coast in 1959. This last fish was left behind by the retreating tide and was very much alive at the time it was found. This, to my mind, is material proof of the existence of very big conger in inshore waters. I would strongly advise keen conger fishermen to survey thoroughly the likely marks close to the shore before pinning their hopes on distant deep-water grounds. I suspect that conger, living in areas where no one suspects their presence, eventually die of old age or become too feeble to feed themselves properly, and so drift ashore, either as fresh corpses or in a severely-weakened condition.

Stories about giant conger are common, every harbour, pier or estuary has its local version. Most of these can be taken with a pinch of the proverbial salt but some, without a shadow of doubt, are based on absolute truth. There are, for example, massive conger in the estuary of the Fowey river, Cornwall. Fish of similar size once existed around the lighthouse quay at Mevagissey in Cornwall. Monster conger also live in the mouth of the Tamar river in the Plymouth area.

Several of the old harbour walls on the west coast of Ireland shelter eels of almost unbelievable size. And what of Scotland? Little has been written about conger fishing in Scottish waters, but there are still plenty of conger there and some pretty huge ones at that; a 101 lb (45.3 kg) eel was caught in a prawn trawl off St Abbs' Head.

Over the past twenty years I have made a study of big conger in inshore waters and conclude that conger will grow to record-breaking size in comparatively shallow inshore areas, if the area in question provides them with shelter and a regular supply of food. Some Cornish harbours, for example, contain conger of great size which live in various holes along the outer quay wall. These fish are assured of a regular supply of food, for the long-line boats dump both their unused bait and the entrails from their catches into the harbour after each trip. The resident conger, therefore, get a maximum amount of food with a minimum amount of effort, with the result that they grow at a remarkably fast rate. I have had conger to nearly 50 lb (22.6 kg) while harbour fishing and have hooked and lost much larger specimens. One huge eel even smashed a special rod and twisted the seat of my large reel in a straight run. The line held despite the fact that the rod parted and the reel buckled, but I was powerless to stop the fish from slithering under some immovable obstruction and I was finally forced to break the line by hand. I quote this to illustrate the kind of situation that can occur when conger have plenty of cover and a consistent supply of food literally dumped on their doorstep. The Scottish fishing harbours, where commercial fishing is still very much alive, are an obvious place to expect to find big conger close inshore. Most of these harbours are as yet untouched. True conger fishing being a southern sport.

Although they are not a shoaling species, they are gregarious, and large numbers of eels of all sizes will live in close proximity to one another in apparent harmony. The females grow to a much greater size than the males. It is a widespread belief that outsize specimens are usually barren females which, being unable to spawn, feed continuously right up until the time they die; as all the large congers found either dead or dying have been in reasonable condition, this seems to indicate that death strikes mature eels very rapidly. Conger can be caught at almost any time of the year, but the late summer and autumn months usually fish the best. It is a popular fallacy that conger are 'dirty' feeders living, for the most part, on rotten fish gleaned from the sea bed. This is nonsense. As a general rule, conger are much less inclined to eat stale food than skate or ray. Although I have caught conger on a stinking bait, I have always found stale baits to be inferior to fresh ones when conger were the quarry.

Tackle

In my opinion, it is almost impossible to over-estimate the strength of a very large conger. Far too many anglers make the mistake of seriously under-estimating the terrific power of these eels. There is nothing on the British list more capable of showing up a weakness or defect in tackle than an enraged conger, and yet, anglers still insist on going boat fishing with what they consider to be sporting tackle. My advice is to forget any preconceived idea about conger being a sporting species which should be given a fair opportunity. Under no circumstances should light or medium tackle be used for hunting big conger. Conger fight in a completely different way from all other fish, making it impossible to play them in a conventional fashion. Sheer brute force is the only tactic likely to beat a big conger, so don't make the mistake of hooking a record breaker on tackle that won't stand the punishment. My advice is to fish heavy and think in terms of records. Choice of tackle depends on two things: where you intend to fish and the size of the conger you may hook. For wreck fishing, use 80 lb (36.2 kg) class gear, a hollow-glass shark-type rod matched with a large capacity multiplier holding a minimum of 300 yards (275 m) of 80 lb (36.2 kg) breaking-strain nylon line. This may sound ridiculously strong but it is not over-heavy when it comes to forcing a big eel out from some solid underwater obstruction. Even a 30 lb (13.6 kg) eel, with its broad tail firmly wrapped round a snag, can test this sort of tackle to the utmost and a large eel can exert enough brute strength to snap a line like this without undue effort. For less snaggy areas where the average eel weighs 15–30 lb (6.8–13.6 kg) a lighter set of tackle can be used. For example, where conger of over 40 lb (18.1 kg) are uncommon, most keen congermen use a medium-weight boat fishing outfit and line of 35 or 50 lb (15.8 or 22.6 kg) breaking strain.

My advice would be to make a habit of fishing heavier than usual when after conger. Monster fish are not commonly encountered; but it is worth being prepared for the eventuality. There is no question of being unfair to conger by using line with a breaking strain of twice the weight of the average fish, as I said earlier, fighting a conger of any reasonable size is a matter of brute strength rather than skill, and the only tactic worth using is the one that uses the rod, line and reel as a lifting device rather than as a buffer against which the eel can exhaust its strength. A conger rarely attempts to run when it feels the hook. The only exception being on the rare occasion a conger is hooked well away from its stronghold. Normally, however, it will be in or close to its retreat when it takes the bait. The moment the hook is set, use rod and reel to drag the eel as far off the seabed as possible. The first few seconds of battle are really critical when fighting a conger. Once it gets its head down it has every chance of going to ground and breaking the line; but, if it can be lifted and pumped up well clear of the bottom there is a good chance that it will be successfully boated.

A conger hauled out of its natural habitat fights in a way peculiar to itself. Instead of running, it performs intricate figure of eight movements, jagging its big head about in a desperate attempt to loosen the hook. If this fails, it starts to spin, gradually increasing its speed as it nears the surface – an added reason for using extra-heavy gear at all times.

Tackle (Shore)

As already stated, there is no finesse about conger fishing and the shore angler who wishes to fish light should forget about conger and concentrate on some other fish. Although choice of shore tackle is, to some extent, a matter of personal preference, far too many anglers believe that any old tackle will do for congering, which is one reason why so many breakages occur.

Rods

Hollow glass or carbon rods have superseded rods of all other rod-making materials, and the conger enthusiast has a multitude of suitable rods to choose from. It is sensible to review local venues before purchasing a rod, then choose the rod accordingly. A good conger rod should be strong, yet flexible enough to cast a big bait accurately. Its fittings must be good quality and robust, as a conger rod takes a lot of hard knocks over the years and inferior fittings are quick to crack or corrode. For general use I would recommend an 11 or 12 ft (3.3 or 3.6 m) hollow glass beachcaster, capable of throwing weights of 8–12 oz (0.22–0.34 kg).

Reels

Only one type of reel is of any practical use for shore fishing for conger. This is the multiplier. There are, of course, plenty of multiplying reels available, but always remember that a conger reel has to hold at least 200 yards/metres of 25–30 lb (11.3–13.6 kg) breaking-strain line so make sure the drum is large enough to take the heavy line. Reels with metal spools are best when using plain nylon line, as nylon contracts under pressure and will crack a plastic spool. Fixed-spool reels are of no use whatever for conger fishing; although easy to cast, their limited-line capacity make them impractical. The bale-arm mechanism is also liable to snap or twist under strain, which makes them unreliable when pitted against the brute strength of a big conger.

Lines

Conger live among thick jagged rock, the kind of bottom which will quickly destroy a line. Because of this, I prefer to use plain nylon for conger fishing as, even in the heavier breaking strains, it is comparatively inexpensive and therefore expendable. The main drawback with heavy nylon is that it has a natural elasticity which occasionally leads to a lost fish.

Traces

A nylon-covered braided wire of 40–50 lb (18.1–22.6 kg) breaking strain is the best trace material as yet available. This can be bought by the coil and traces can be made up at home, which is cheaper than buying factory-made traces: The beauty of the home-made trace is that it can be made to suit your own requirements. A special crimping tool and suitable crimps (see Fig. 32) should be purchased, so that the trace can be neatly and securely finished off. A good conger trace should incorporate at least two swivels. These will help to eliminate any kinks the spinning eel puts into the trace as it fights for its life. I would advise every conger angler to use a plated-steel hook, size 6-0, 8-0 or 10-0, sharpened with a carborundum stone. The ideal hook has an offset point (see Fig. 33) which makes it ideal for bony-mouthed fish like conger. One of these hooks on a 3 ft (0.9 m) length of double-swivelled wire (see Fig. 34) is ideal for all forms of conger fishing. The wire should have a breaking strain equal to the breaking strain of the actual reel line. It pays to check the trace after each fish has been caught. The easiest way of checking that the wire is undamaged is to run it through the fingers once or twice: a trace should be changed at the slightest sign of damage, as weak spots usually break under pressure.

(Fig. 32)

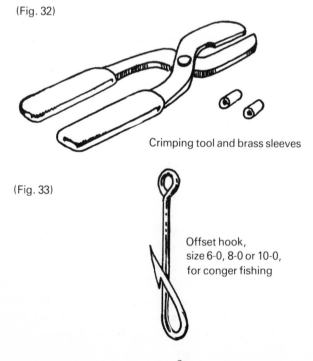

Crimping tool and brass sleeves

(Fig. 33)

Offset hook,
size 6-0, 8-0 or 10-0,
for conger fishing

60

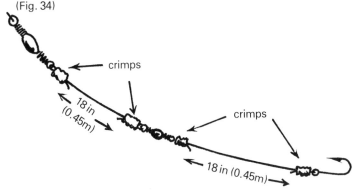

(Fig. 34)

crimps

18 in (0.45m)

crimps

18 in (0.45m)

Double-swivelled wire trace

Wreck men fish heavier, making and using traces of fencing wire. Even these crude traces are occasionally broken; proof of the power that a huge eel can bring to bear on terminal tackle.

Methods

Legering is the best boat/shore fishing method to use for conger, and it is essential that the line should run easily through the lead link as conger are wary fish, despite their large size and great strength, and will eject a bait the moment they detect any additional drag on the line. Conger are true bottom feeders, so the bait should rest right on the seabed. Because of this, it is advisable to use a short trace between lead and hook. In fact, most experienced congermen allow the first trace swivel to act as a stop for the lead link. To avoid the possibility of this fouling up, I use a 2 in (5 cm) length of polythene tube and two large plastic beads between the lead and the trace swivel (see Fig. 35). A normal conger trace is 2½ ft-3 ft (0.76-0.9 m) long, which gives ample distance between lead and bait. Longer traces can be a drawback; in a strong tide, a long trace will allow the bait to lift from the bottom. The line between rod tip and lead should be kept taut at all times. Conger are delicate feeders and if there is any slack in the line, preliminary bites will go undetected.

Because conger live close to rocks or other solid obstructions, tackle loss during a conger session can be very high. Most 'hang ups' occur when the lead (rather than the reel line or wire trace) becomes jammed in a crevice. To cut tackle loss to a minimum, it pays to attach the lead to a few inches of line of a lesser breaking strain than the actual reel line. In the north of England this is known as 'rotten-bottom tackle'. A swivel can be used as a sliding link (see Fig. 36) so that, if the lead does become snagged up, the weaker line will snap under rod pressure leaving the reel line and trace intact.

(Fig. 35)

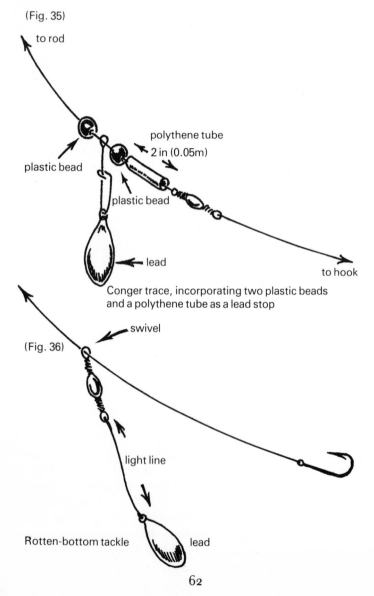

to rod

polythene tube
2 in (0.05m)

plastic bead

plastic bead

lead

to hook

Conger trace, incorporating two plastic beads
and a polythene tube as a lead stop

swivel

(Fig. 36)

light line

Rotten-bottom tackle   lead

The best conger bait is undoubtedly a large chunk of fresh squid or cuttlefish. Small imported squid can also be used, though these are seldom as effective as fresh-caught baits. Some anglers believe that squid baits should be thoroughly pounded with a wooden mallet before use. Conger are said to be attracted to 'tenderised' baits of this type. I doubt the validity of this theory. Conger have wide ranging appetites and almost any type of fresh fish can be turned into bait. Oily-fleshed baits such as mackerel, pilchard or herring are probably the best, because conger hunt by scent as much as by sight. An oil slick exuding from a bait will attract any eels in the vicinity. When very big conger are known to frequent a particular mark, it is advisable to use a large bait. Big conger, like most heavy fish, tend to be lazy and are more inclined to swallow one large offering rather than have to work hard at picking up a number of small baits. For conger of average size, one good mackerel should make three baits (see Fig. 37). A fillet bait from the side of a fish should be lashed to your line, above the eye of the hook, with a length of elastic thread (see Fig. 38), so that the bait doesn't slide down the hook shank and bunch up on the bend of the hook. A badly presented bait seldom catches fish: particularly big conger.

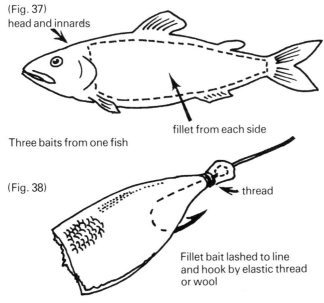

(Fig. 37)
head and innards

fillet from each side

Three baits from one fish

(Fig. 38)

thread

Fillet bait lashed to line and hook by elastic thread or wool

When cutting fish baits for conger, care should be taken to remove the head with the guts still attached. This makes a deadly bait for conger (and for most other large bottom-feeding fish as well). The softness and the smell of the hanging guts are, without doubt, the main attraction of this bait. Whole small pouting, pollack and wrasse make good conger baits. These can be used either alive or dead. Dead baits should be hooked through the wrist of the tail, and their side scored diagonally with a sharp thin-bladed knife. This will allow the juice of the bait to form a scent trail that the fish can follow. Live baits should be hooked through the upper lip so that they hold their position facing into the flow of water. A bait hooked in this fashion will remain alive for a considerable period. Conger are active hunters and catch most of their food alive.

Groundbait

It has been proved that conger of all sizes are attracted by groundbait, and it should be used whenever conditions allow. It is common practice in many boat-fishing areas to fasten a mesh bag full of mashed-up fish to the anchor before throwing it over the side (see **Fig. 39**). The only drawback to this is that when there is an extra-strong tide running, and there is a lot of rope between the boat and anchor, conger tend to concentrate well in front of the angler's bait. Shore fishermen can ground-bait an area by chopping fish and throwing the cuttings into the sea. I put my groundbait into a paper bag, add a stone, screw up the neck of the bag and drop it into the sea: the bag breaks up when it reaches the bottom and this allows the groundbait to drift away with the tide flow.

(Fig. 39)

A mesh bag (rubby dubby) can be attached to the anchor to provide groundbait

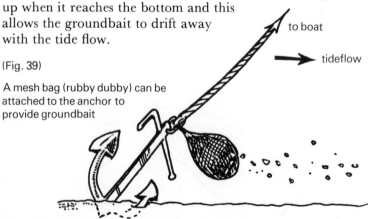

to boat

tideflow

Bites

Conger of all sizes are inclined to play with their bait for some time before actually taking it into their mouths. Normally, the bigger the fish the gentler it will be with the bait; very small conger rattle the rod tip as they mouth at the bait. Many anglers lose conger by striking too soon at a taking fish – a natural reflex action – but where conger are concerned, patience is essential. The first indication that a conger has found the bait normally comes when the rod tip is slowly pulled down and then released. As soon as this initial movement is felt, the rod tip should be lowered to give the hungry fish a little line to play with. At the same time, it is advisable to disengage the reel spool so the biting eel can take additional line freely as it takes up the slack line. In this way, the fish can be induced to take the bait properly. The exception to this rule comes when wreck fishing. Instant strikes are then essential. Give a wreck-eel line and it will back up under cover, leaving the angler to break off his terminal tackle. *Strike and lift, lift and crank the reel handle*, is the technique for wrecking. Simple and brutal, but it works! Conger never appear to be in much of a hurry with a bait. As much as ten minutes may elapse between the time of the first bite indication and the time when the eel can be felt moving off with the bait. To avoid dragging the bait away from the eel, the strike must be made when the fish actually begins to run out line. Provided that one is prepared to relax and ignore the first twitchy bites, hooking a conger is a simple enough operation, but it is surprising just how many anglers are unable to control their instinctive striking reactions and so lose their fish by pulling the bait away from it.

Handling conger

How you boat a hooked conger depends on the size and freeboard of the boat you are fishing from. On a large charter boat with plenty of deck space, the thrashing eel can be gaffed inboard and dropped on to the deck or into a large fish container. Conger and shallow-fish boxes do not go together. An eel will soon get its strong tail over the rim of the box and lever its body on to the deck. Because of this, most charter boats are equipped with plastic dustbins which are deep enough to hold average eels without fear of them escaping. For small boat

65

work, however, there is usually no room for a bulky container of the dustbin type. Under such circumstances, it is best to drop the eel straight into a strong heavy-duty sack. The hook trace should be cut from the reel line, so that the fish can be unhooked ashore where one has plenty of space to work. Under no circumstances should conger be allowed to lie loose in the bottom of a small boat. Their body slime will quickly make the boat as slippery as an ice rink, and a slip on a small boat may well cause a fatal accident. The sight of a writhing conger stirs many anglers to an excitement probably motivated by their fear of the fish. Invariably their first reaction is to grasp the nearest blunt instrument and try to kill the fish. This can be dangerous, especially in dinghy-type boats. More than one angler has missed his target and stove in the bottom of his boat. This may appear to have its funny side, but it happens more frequently than most people realise and the results can be serious.

My advice is to leave the conger alone. Only remove the trace if the hook is in the lip of the fish and never attempt to probe down an eel's throat to extract tackle. 'Dead' eels have a nasty habit of suddenly coming to life and the tooth-filled jaws of a reasonably large eel can easily remove your fingers.

I may seem to be overstressing the dangers involved. But remember that an accident at sea is far more dangerous than one on land, for the victim is a long way from hospital or help of any kind.

A strong gaff should be carried in the boat at all times.

Gaffing a conger

The only practical method of bringing a conger ashore is to gaff it and lift it bodily from the sea in one clean movement. There are many kinds of gaff available. Many are unsuitable for conger, being too flimsy to stand the terrific pressures imposed upon them. Extendable gaffs come into the unsuitable category for, although a telescopic handle can be useful, they lack the necessary strength to deal with a decent conger and snap or bend under the strain. Remember that a gaffed conger does not lie still on the gaff. It twists and contorts its body and generally tries to lever itself off the steel hook and only a strong gaff head will stand up to this sort of pressure. I prefer to purchase a gaff head (see Fig. 40) and lash it securely to a length of stout blackthorn. Having lashed it to the handle as tightly as possible I

66

then apply several coats of marine varnish to the cord whipping, so that the cord contracts and makes a neat, water-resistant job. Blackthorn is the ideal material for a gaff handle; it is tough, springy and capable of standing up to a heavy weight without splitting or snapping at a crucial time. The gaff point should be honed to a sharp point; when not in use, it should be covered by a cork. I like to gaff my conger just behind the head but other anglers prefer to gaff them through the middle of their bodies. This is a personal choice but, whichever method you use, get the eel out of the water as swiftly as possible for they are quick to lever themselves off the gaff.

(Fig. 40)

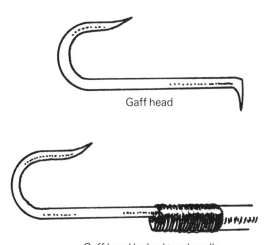

Gaff head

Gaff head lashed to a handle

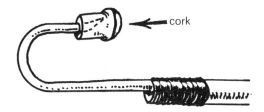

cork

When not in use the point of a gaff must be covered with a cork

Controlling a large eel is no easy matter when it is thrashing about on slippery weed-covered rocks. Some anglers sever the backbone of the eel with a sharp knife or chop off its head with a hand axe. Neither method is practical and anyone who tries these tactics is more likely to kill himself than kill his catch. The two items I find most useful for controlling conger are a mallet and a large heavy-duty polythene bag (of the type used to hold fertiliser). The mallet is an ideal weapon for conger, and one heavy blow on an eel's snout is normally sufficient to stun it for long enough to extract the hook or cut the trace and drop the fish into a bag. A sack can be used but the polythene bag is easier to keep clean, an important consideration, for stale conger slime has a stink almost beyond belief. It is always best to go conger fishing with at least one companion; rocks are tricky places to fish from at the best of times, and after dark they are doubly dangerous, particularly when fish as large and powerful as conger are the quarry. Although I have caught many conger from rock marks and am used to gaffing and handling big eels single-handed, there have been many occasions when I would have welcomed some help. So be wise and fish with company whenever possible.

The effects of weather on conger

The best time to catch conger on inshore grounds is on a very warm, dark night. If the sky is overcast with little or no wind, good sport can almost be guaranteed. Inshore conger are, almost exclusively, nocturnal feeders; but over deep-water marks, the fish can be expected to feed at all times of the day, presumably because light does not penetrate water beyond a certain depth.

Conger are usually uninclined to feed on cold, clear nights, and in shallow water a sudden snap of frosty weather will often kill off most of the resident eels. Most of the large conger washed up dead or dying have been found during the winter months.

Flounder and Flatfish

Despite their small average size, flounder are one of the most popular sea fish in the British Isles. Many expert anglers have devoted their entire angling careers to the study of flounder and the methods required to catch them. Probably the greatest devotee of flounder fishing was the late J P Garrard (*Seangler*), who wrote a book entitled *Sea Angling with the Baited Spoon*, published 1960, a book which all sea anglers would be well advised to read and digest.

Flounder can be caught at practically any time of the year, though the winter months are best. Flounders can be regarded as real cold-weather fish, and they will often feed in sea temperatures so low that nothing else will stir itself to look at a bait. I have been out in a boat, fishing the Solent estuaries and tidal creeks in Hampshire when the marsh grass and sedge were white with frost, and still caught good flounder. I have finally reached the conclusion that the colder it is the more active flounder become.

These fish have a wide distribution and can be found all round Britain and Ireland. They show a marked liking for fresh or brackish water, and often gather in harbours, creeks and estuaries. Flounder will also travel considerable distances up river, and there are records of them being caught far inland.

The flounder is a small thick-bodied flatfish. Its head and mouth are large and it has powerful jaws armed with sharp conical teeth. In colour it varies considerably from one locality to another. The back of the fish is usually greyish-brown, but I have seen many darker specimens. In fact, flounder change their colour to suit their surroundings. I have taken large flounder, while boat fishing a Cornish estuary, which had a sprinkling of orange spots on their backs. At first sight, I mistook the fish for medium-sized plaice, but found that as they died the spots disappeared. A close inspection showed that my fish were true flounder – and very large ones at that. Freak flounder are very common. Although the underparts are usually white, I have seen specimens which were marked on both sides.

The average weight of rod-caught flounder is about $\frac{3}{4}$ lb (0.33 kg) but specimens of over 4 lb (1.8 kg) do occur. Flounder are active fish which live mainly on crustacea, worms and small fish. They also eat small shore crabs and sand shrimps.

Tackle

For bottom fishing from a boat in deep water, a light boat-fishing outfit can be used, although it will not give the fish much opportunity to show fight.

For all-round fishing, a 7 or 8 ft (2.1 or 2.4 m) light hollow-glass spinning rod is best. This should be used in conjunction with a medium sized fixed-spool reel loaded with nylon line of 8 or 10 lb (3.6 or 4.5 kg) breaking strain. This outfit will do for both bottom fishing and spinning. Long casting is often an essential part of boat fishing for flounder. To ensure that this can be achieved with the minimum of effort, the reel spool should be loaded with line to within $\frac{1}{8}$ in (3 mm) of the spool lip. Where a reel with an exceptionally deep spool is used, a suitable length of old line can be wound on first and used as backing for the new line.

A standard beachcasting rod can be used for general flounder fishing from the shore. The lighter the rod the better it will be. I use an 11 ft (3.3 m) bass rod designed to cast a maximum of 4 oz (0.11 kg) of lead. Choice of reel is up to the individual: a large sized fixed-spool reel or a beach-sized multiplier can be used.

Methods

Although flounder can be caught on a static leger or wander type of tackle, the most successful and most widely used method is the baited-spoon technique. This was devised by J P Garrard for flounder fishing in Langstone Harbour but has become a standard technique all round British coasts.

Baited spoon

This, without doubt, is the most deadly method yet devised for catching flounder. Flounder spoons are now available in great numbers. I have always found that larger spoons make the best fish catchers, my own choice being a 2½–3 in (6.3–7.5 cm) white-plastic or silver-metal spoon (see Fig. 41). As can be seen from the diagram, the hook should trail from 1½–2 in (3.8–5 cm) behind the spoon. This distance is critical. Spoons fitted with longer hook-trails rarely catch fish in any quantity although, on occasion, I have caught both plaice and flounder on a spoon with an 18 in (0.45 m) trail.

Flounder cannot be regarded as a truly predatory species, so why does the sight of a spoon (which is obviously designed to simulate the movement of a small fish) drive flounder to such a frenzy? As it is rare for flounder to attack an unbaited spoon, it is possible that flounder see the baited spoon as a very small flatfish making off with a largish worm. The immediate re-action of an adult flounder would be to give chase, to steal away the worm in much the same way that other animals will steal food from one another.

A spoon I have used to good effect on flounder is a Rauto ice-fishing spoon, manufactured in Sweden. The only drawback to this lure is its price, which is approximately twice that of an English-made flounder spoon. The Rauto is a very good attractor, particularly in unclear water. In estuaries that carry a lot of flood water, a copper-coloured spoon attracts and catches fish better than any other lure.

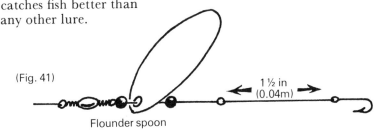

(Fig. 41)

1½ in (0.04m)

Flounder spoon

Trolling with baited spoon

Trolling a baited spoon behind a slowly moving boat is an ex-tremely good way of catching flounder. I have trolled these baits at various speeds, but I have noticed that I always catch more fish when the spoon is working slowly, just off the bottom. It is

71

essential at all times to troll *with* the current, for this is the way flatfish normally swim and feed. A bait working against the tide will appear unnatural to the fish and may scare them away. Most baited-spoon specialists fish alone from small rowing boats. Obviously, they cannot row and hold a rod at the same time, so the rod has to be laid down so that its tip projects over the stern. When a flounder or other flatfish strikes at the bait, the rod tip will give a clear indication of the bite, allowing the angler plenty of time to put down the oars and pick up the rod. Never strike at the first sign of a bite. Flounder like to trail along behind the spoon, gently nibbling at the bait. Once a fish is certain that there is no danger, it will take the bait and hook confidently, dragging the rod tip hard down as it moves away (see Fig. 42). The fish will usually hook itself, but it pays to strike, just to make certain. Trolling can only be done from a moving boat. Without doubt, it is the best way to catch flounder, for the bait can be shown to the fish over a wide area and each hot-spot can be covered.

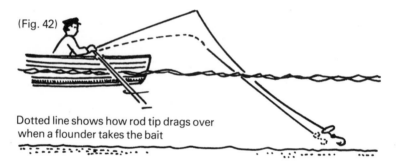

(Fig. 42)

Dotted line shows how rod tip drags over when a flounder takes the bait

Spinning with baited spoon

Not all anglers want to spend their time rowing a boat for hours on end. Fortunately the baited-spoon technique can be adapted for use from an anchored boat or for shore fishing.

When spinning from a static position, it is essential to remember that, to work correctly, the baited spoon must be cast up-current and worked back with the run of the tide. Flatfish rarely snatch bait that is working against or across the prevailing flow of water, so there is little point in casting anywhere other than up-current. To get the best out of this type of fishing, it is advisable to adopt a roving style of angling, moving from one place to another, stopping for a dozen or so casts at each likely spot and, if the bites are not forthcoming, moving on.

Float-fished spoons

The float-fished spoon (see Fig. 43) is an adaptation of the standard flounder-spoon technique. Although it is a rather limited method it sometimes brings a good bag of fish. To get the most out of this type of terminal rig, the tackle should be cast as far up-tide as possible and worked back towards the angler. Failing this, it can be allowed to drift down the current. The only place I have seen this method used consistently is at the mouth of the Lymington river in Hampshire but I can see no reason why it should not fish just as well elsewhere.

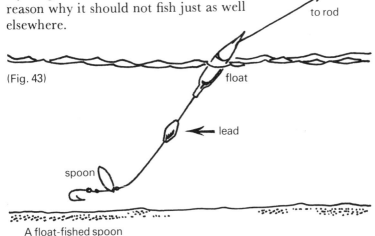

(Fig. 43)

to rod

float

lead

spoon

A float-fished spoon

Bottom fishing

Flounder and other small flatfish can be caught on the bottom tackle described in the following section.

Plaice

The plaice is one of the best-known flatfish and, owing to its qualities as a table fish, it is much sought after by anglers. Its eyes and coloured half are on its right side and like most 'flatties' it varies in colour from one locality to another; a typical specimen being browny-coloured on the eye side, with white underparts. The back is heavily spotted with large orange or red blotches. Plaice have been caught to over 8 lb (3.6 kg) but the average fish weighs between 1½ and 2 lb (0.7 and 0.9 kg). Any plaice of over 5 lb (2.3 kg) can be regarded as a really good catch.

Unlike flounder, plaice are a summer species. They have a wide distribution and are found around most of the British Isles. They are commonest in areas where the sea bed is comprised of sand, mud or shell grit.

Unfortunately, extensive inshore trawling has ruined many of the best plaice grounds. Most of the big fish now caught on rod and line are taken from sheltered inshore marks where trawlers cannot work. Shellfish, particularly mussels, form the basic diet of the adult plaice, but marine worms, shrimps, soft crabs, small fish and starfish are also eaten. Large plaice can be caught in many areas. Poole Harbour, in Dorset, was once the most famous big-plaice venue in Britain; but constant over fishing has taken its toll and catches are now on the decline, although some huge fish are still caught annually from marks around Brownsea Island. I think that, in time, Scottish waters will become the new Mecca of the ardent plaice fishermen. Marks off the Isle of Arran, and the sea lochs of the Western Highlands, are alive with plaice – some of them very big fish indeed.

Tackle

Choice of tackle for plaice fishing depends on the area you intend to fish. For example, the type of tackle described for flounder can be adapted for plaice fishing in most sheltered estuaries. Offshore marks, or grounds subjected to a considerable flow of tide, call for much heavier tackle. Even so, a standard light boat rod should suffice under most conditions. My advice would be to fish as light as conditions will allow. In this way you will catch more fish, and get more sport, than you would if you used typical heavy boat gear. For most boat fishing a 6 or 12 lb (2.7 or 5.4 kg) class rod is ideal.

Terminal tackle

Many plaice anglers fish multiple-hook rigs, for when the fish are in a feeding mood it is possible to take them two or three at a time. The most popular all-round flatfish tackle is the three-hook paternoster trot (see Fig. 44). Each plaice area has its own adaptation of the original idea. For example, off the Kent coast, anglers catch plaice on elaborate paternosters which incorporate two wire or plastic booms set one on top of the other directly above the lead (see Fig. 45).

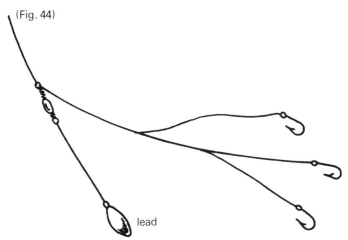

(Fig. 44)

lead

The three-hook paternoster trot for plaice

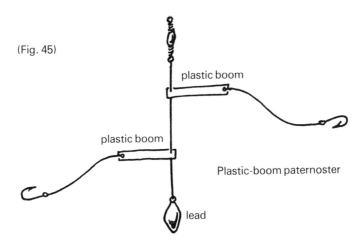

(Fig. 45)

plastic boom

plastic boom

Plastic-boom paternoster

lead

A basic single-hook or double-hook running leger can, obviously, be used for plaice fishing; but in many estuary waters, where plaice are common, fishing is regularly ruined by bait-robbing shore crabs which get to the bait before the fish have a chance to find it. The only practical way of overcoming this is to use a floating leger (see Fig. 46). This is by no means the best way to catch plaice, but the cork will keep the bait off the sea-bed and out of range of a crab and plaice are not averse to taking a bait that is suspended in this way.

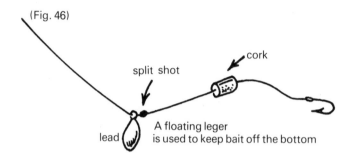

(Fig. 46)

cork

split shot

lead

A floating leger is used to keep bait off the bottom

Wander tackle (see Fig. 47) is the favourite terminal tackle of most plaice specialists. As its name implies, it is designed to roll slowly over the sea bed, searching out the bottom as it goes. To work properly, wander tackle can only be used on a clean, snagfree bottom. It is rigged as for a normal leger, except that, instead of using a lead that would hold the bait in one position, say 8 oz (0.22 kg), a weight of only 4 oz (0.11 kg) should be used, so that the movement of the tide rolls or bounces the bait slowly over the seabed. To fish this method correctly, the rod must be held at all times, so that line can be smoothly paid off the reel as the tackle rolls away from the boat. As can be seen from the diagram, the weight should be split into two equal portions, so that the tackle runs out without becoming tangled. I normally use spiral leads for this tackle, because often I find it necessary to increase or decrease the amount of lead to suit the changing flow of the tide. This can be achieved by unwinding a spiral lead and substituting the lead required. Once the line has been wrapped around the spiral grooves on the lead, the weight should be bent so that it cannot slide up the line (see Fig. 48).

When bottom fishing for plaice, or other small flatfish, narrow-gape long-shanked size 1 or 2 hooks should be used.

(Fig. 47)

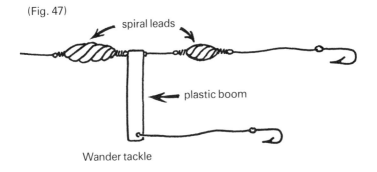

spiral leads

← plastic boom

Wander tackle

(Fig. 48)

to rod

to hook

A spiral lead should be bent to stop it sliding up the line

Other flatfish

Dab, sole, witch, megrim, scaldfish and topknot can all be caught on rod and line. Bottom fishing is the only successful method to use for these fish and no special tackle or tactics are required to catch them. Dab and sole are the commonest, but I have caught a number of megrim while bottom fishing in Scottish waters.

Turbot

A turbot is a real prize catch. For its large size, beautifully marked back and excellent taste make it a much sought-after fish. Large turbot seem to hold a strange fascination for many anglers. Each season, the lure of these large predatory flatfish brings anglers from all over the British Isles to such places as Coverack, Dartmouth and Weymouth; for it is from marks off these ports that most of the big turbot are landed. The Varne

Bank, off Dover, has long been noted for its magnificent turbot fishing but, unfortunately, the strength of the local tide makes rod-and-line fishing practically impossible at most times of the year.

Owing to its large average size, it is difficult to confuse the turbot with other members of the flatfish family (with the possible exception of brill). The eyes and the coloured half of the turbot are on the upper or left-hand side of its body. Its back is normally greyish-brown, with a thick freckling of darker spots and blotches. Colouration is variable, depending, to a great extent, on what sort of seabed the fish was feeding over when caught.

Turbot are normally caught during the spring and summer months, but they can be taken at almost any time of the year in very deep water. Turbot undoubtedly have a wide distribution but, from the rod-and-line man's point of view, they are most common in southern waters, although they are nomadic, and odd specimens turn up in the most unexpected places. For example, a 13 lb (5.9 kg) fish was caught at Golant, well up the Fowey River; a 27 lb (12.2 kg) specimen was caught by a mullet-angler, fishing from the lighthouse quay at Mevagissey; and a 21 lb (9.5 kg) turbot was recently caught by a small-boat angler, less than 150 yards (137 m) out from the beach at Bournemouth, Dorset. As a general rule, however, the angler wishing to catch turbot in quantity must go to a known turbot ground and fish it properly before he or she can hope to catch these handsome fish.

Big turbot like to live and feed in fast and heavy water. A prime example of this is the Shambles Bank, off Weymouth, once the most famous big-turbot mark in the country and still good for large fish. Shambles fishermen regularly use 4 or 5 lb (1.8 or 2.3 kg) leads to hold their bait on the bottom, and this calls for correspondingly heavy rods, reels and lines. Big baits are also essential. Turbot are true predators, with big mouths and sharp teeth that are ideally suited to catch and hold any bait-sized fish unfortunate enough to come within reach. Turbot reach a weight of at least 35 lb (15.8 kg), but a rod-and-line fisherman who catches a 20 lb (9.1 kg) turbot can be proud of his catch. The last big turbot I caught came from the Portrush area of Northern Ireland. An area which has produced some magnificent fishing in recent seasons.

Tackle

On light tackle, turbot are a sporting proposition. But in many turbot areas, where extra-strong tides prevail at all times, turbot fishermen are forced to employ very heavy gear, in an attempt to offset the huge leads they are forced to use to hold the bait on the bottom. Fortunately, it is now possible to use lighter lead weights by using wire lines. These are a boon to any angler who regularly fishes strong tides. By using a light lead, it is possible accordingly to scale down all the other items of tackle, and so give the fish a chance to show its sporting ability.

My own choice of turbot tackle, for use with wire line, is a medium-weight boat rod with multiplier to match. The breaking strain of the line should be 30–35 lb (13.6–15.8 kg), and at least 200 yards/metres should be used, so that the baited tackle can be worked well out from the stern of the boat. Remember, however, that the rod must be fitted with a roller-tip ring if wire is going to be used; otherwise, a severe tangle will occur the first time the tackle is reeled up from the bottom.

Anglers who, for one reason or another, do not wish to use wire lines will have to step up their tackle accordingly. A heavier rod will be necessary, and reels smaller than the Penn Super Mariner will probably be impractical. Frankly, the angler who wishes to buy a new set of tackle for turbot fishing should purchase a wire-line outfit in the first instance.

Hooks

Turbot have huge mouths, so it pays to use a large hook and a big bait. A Mustad flat-forged 6-o or 8-o is about the best size and type of hook to use. Make absolutely certain that the hook is sharp before use, and check its point for sharpness throughout the day: blunt hooks lead to lost fish.

Traces

Turbot have sharp teeth, so do not make the mistake of using a light trace. The sharp teeth and the sheer bulk of a hooked turbot will soon wear through the line directly above the hook. Nylon-covered wire, with a breaking strain of about 40 lb (18.1 kg), is the ideal material for a turbot trace. Like the hook, this trace should be checked at regular intervals, and discarded at the first sign of wear.

The simplest way to check for faults in nylon-covered wire is to run it through the fingers. Any rough spots or cuts are easily detected. One problem is that once the wire inside the nylon is exposed to the corrosive action of the sea, it rapidly loses its strength, and can often be snapped by hand. Some turbot specialists prefer to use a length of nylon line, with a breaking strain of 60 lb (27.1 kg), as a trace, the reason being that they feel plain nylon is more supple than wire and allows the bait to work in a more natural manner. I do not subscribe to this view, as I feel that heavy nylon tends to become rather stiff and springy in water. Moreover, a heavy nylon trace often loses a great deal of its strength when stored on a line winder and, although it still appears to be strong, it will often break under pressure.

Methods

A plain sliding leger is the best terminal tackle to choose for turbot fishing. Many charter-boat skippers who specialise in taking out turbot-fishing parties prefer to drift their boats over the most likely ground. Others are equally sure that an anchored boat produces the best overall results. In either case, a running leger is the ideal form of terminal tackle.

I use a long link between lead and hook, so that the bait can work with the flow of the tide. Turbot, like other fish which hunt actively, are attracted by movement. They prefer a moving bait rather than one which remains static.

Dead sand eels, sprats, small mackerel and long fish-fillets are the most widely used turbot bait; but, if you can get them, small live pouting, dab or large sand eels are far superior to deadbait, no matter how fresh the deadbait may be. I am always surprised at how few sea anglers fish with livebait. I have seen anglers catch and kill mackerel and pouting, then put the bait back on the hook, without thinking that if left alive, the bait would make a much more attractive mouthful to a hunting fish. More and more anglers are experimenting with live baits, with the result that some very large fish are now being caught.

Livebait should be hooked only through the upper jaw in heavy tides, so that they can swim and move as naturally as possible with the tide flow. Bait hooked through the back or wrist of the tail turn broadside on to the flow and die as the water floods back through their gills.

1 Bass fishing, Portmellon, South Cornwall *(top)*.

2 Rock fishing, North Cornwall *(right)*.

All photographs by Trevor Housby except nos. 14 and 21 (P. Williams).

3 The head of a red bream, note large eyes for feeding in darkness *(left)*.
4 Specimen red bream *(left, inset)*.
5 A fine bass, note the large mouth *(top)*.
6 Spinning for bass, Southern Ireland *(bottom left)*.
7 A 10½ lb (4.8 kg) bass from Cornwall *(bottom centre)*.
8 Casting for bass on a storm beach *(bottom right)*.

9 Cod, ling and pollack are among 2,000 lb (900 kg) of fish for a Hampshire wrecking party *(left)*.

10 A fine cod caught off the Needles, Isle of Wight *(top)*.

11 Cod like a redgill sand eel *(bottom left)*.

12 Large cod have huge mouths *(bottom right)*.

13 A nice codling taken
   on a nasty day *(left)*.

14 A good haddock
   catch, West
   Scotland *(top)*.

15 Specimen haddock,
   County Antrim,
   Northern Ireland
   (right).

16 Fine Channel whiting, Isle of
   Wight *(left)*.

17 A 45 lb (20.5 kg) conger eel *(top
   left)*.

18 Gaffing a conger, Isle of Wight
   (top right).

19 Playing a big conger eel
   (bottom left).

20 A 53 lb (24 kg) conger
   (bottom right).

21 A flounder off Morecambe *(left)*.

22 A plaice, note the distinguishing orange spots *(top)*.

23 A fine turbot caught off Weymouth *(centre)*.

24 Author plus 20 lb (9 kg) turbot *(bottom)*.

25 A nice ling taken off Orkney *(left)*.

26 Catching mackerel on light tackle *(top)*.

27 A string of mackerel *(bottom left)*.

28 Mackerel fishing, Isle of Wight *(bottom right)*.

29 A Christchurch, Dorset, mullet on a spinner *(top)*.

30 Fishing to a shoal of grey mullet *(left)*.

31 A brace of Orkney pollack *(top right)*.

32 Rock fishing for pollack on spinning gear *(bottom right)*.

33 Two pollack for a lady angler *(bottom far right)*.

34 A 150 lb (68 kg) skate, Isle of Wight *(overleaf)*.

35 A nice thornback *(top)*.

36 192 lb (87 kg) skate caught off Orkney *(centre)*.

37 A good Solent sting ray *(bottom)*.

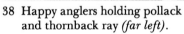

38 Happy anglers holding pollack and thornback ray *(far left)*.

39 A 17 lb (7.7 kg) bull huss from the Isle of Wight ground *(top left)*.

40 A well-hooked tope *(top right)*.

41 Thornback ray, Isle of Wight *(right)*.

42 Author plus 63 lb (28.5 kg) tope from Stranford Lough, N. Ireland *(left)*.

43 A well-marked ballan wrasse *(top)*.

44 Green variant of ballan wrasse *(left)*.

45/46 Male cuckoo wrasse *(centre and bottom right)*.

47 Wrasse fishing from a south Cornish rock mark *(far right)*.

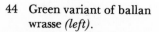

48 A red gurnard *(top left)*.   49 A flectolite jig, ideal for cod fishing *(top right)*.

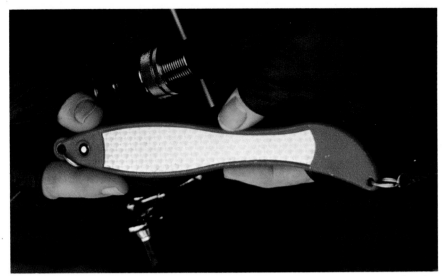

50 The Needles lighthouse, Isle of Wight. A good fishing area *(bottom)*.

51 A sunset rock angler trying for pollack *(overleaf)*.

I have always found turbot bites easy to detect on lightish tackle, but it pays not to strike at the first bite indication. Instead, allow 2 ft (0.3 m) or more of loose line to run off the reel: this will encourage the turbot to swallow the bait quickly. Once it begins to do this, it will make off, dragging the rod tip hard down as it goes. Then, and only then, should you set the hook.

Although turbot put up quite a reasonable fight when hooked on light, well-balanced tackle, they cannot be regarded as a game species.

Whenever turbot anglers congregate, a debate invariably starts as to whether gaff or net should be used to lift beaten turbot out of the water. I believe that if a fish is to be retained, then a gaff should be used, mainly because a gaff is easier to handle than a net, particularly in fast water. Many anglers are against gaffing turbot, on the grounds that the gaff-point ruins the flesh of the fish. I do not agree. A strong but small gaff-hook will do little damage to the fish. Whenever possible, small turbot should be put back alive, and to do this successfully the fish must be netted.

Brill

A brill is smaller than a turbot, although very similar in outward appearance, and large brill are often mistaken for medium-sized turbot. In the past there has been much confusion between the species. The body of an adult brill is more oval than that of a turbot and the upper dorsal fin of a brill extends right down over its eyes; the upper dorsal fin of the turbot is shorter. Like the turbot, the brill varies considerably in colour from one area to another. Generally, the back of the fish is greyish-brown, with a heavy freckling of dark spots and whitish patches. The underside is white, although like most 'flatties' (including turbot), partial colouring on the underside is fairly common.

Brill reach a maximum weight of around 15 lb (6.8 kg), though the average run of fish weighs somewhere between 5–8 lb (2.3–3.2 kg). Brill are probably far more plentiful in English waters than most people realise. Like the turbot, they are commonest off the south and south-west coastline.

Every brill I have caught, or seen caught, has been hooked in fairly deep water. Brill are active fish which live close to the sea bed where they feed, for the most part, on small fish and prawns.

Brill are also fond of lugworms. Many of the big brill are taken by accident, on rag or lugworm baits intended for plaice.

Tackle

Nothing very special in the way of tackle is required to catch brill, and I very much doubt if there is one angler in Britain who goes to sea deliberately to catch this fish. Many brill fall to turbot tackle and are hauled into the boat without being given an opportunity to fight. On light tackle, however, the brill is a sporting proposition.

Plain leger or paternoster trot tackle should be used. These fish like a good-sized live or deadbait. If deadbait is used, it should be as fresh as possible, for brill are not scavengers and seldom take stale bait.

Halibut

Although technically a flatfish, halibut are large and strong enough to be regarded as a game-fishing species. The largest specimen I can trace was taken on a great line. This monster weighed 625 lb (283 kg) when gutted and had an overall length of 9 ft 2 in (2.8 m). This was obviously an exception, but halibut of up to 300 lb (136 kg) have been caught fairly frequently by commercial methods; and halibut up to 234 lb (106 kg) have been caught by British anglers. All halibut caught on rod and line make front-page news in the angling press, for the catching of a halibut is still a rare event and few anglers can claim to have hooked, let alone landed one. As yet, they are still something of a mystery but, with the increase of new sea angling centres in Orkney and Caithness, it is only a matter of a few seasons before more is learned about their movements and feeding habits. Halibut are easy to identify by their vast size, and the body of a halibut is more elongated and more rounded than that of most other flatfish. Their general colour is greenish-brown; the underparts are white; mouth is large and jaws are filled with sharp teeth.

Halibut are a northern species, commonest in arctic or sub-arctic regions. No one yet knows how common these fish are off the north coast of Scotland, but quite a few have been hooked during the past two or three seasons, mainly around the Orkneys. Individual specimens occasionally wander south, though this is rare. At least one fish has been caught in northern Irish waters.

Halibut are solitary creatures which live by catching small coalfish, cod, herrings, skate, lobsters and crabs, in fact practically anything sizeable they can find. Very few anglers have ever caught more than one halibut, and our rather limited knowledge of these fish is based on the few specimens landed.

Tackle

From eye-witness reports, a hooked halibut is a rough-and-tumble fighter with both strength and weight in its favour. Because of this, anglers seriously contemplating spending their time halibut fishing in Scottish waters would be well advised to choose their tackle very carefully indeed. Heavy skate or shark-weight tackle is the best gear to use against large halibut, such as a hollow-glass rod and a large multiplier of the Tatler V type. This should hold at least 400 yards (365 m) of line with an 80 lb (36.2 kg) breaking strain. Most large rod-caught halibut, including Mr Colin Booth's British and World record of 234 lb (106 kg), have been taken on the British-made Tatler range of reels.

Terminal tackle should be equally strong, and 10-0 and 12-0 hooks are essential. Baits should be large and preferably alive. An alternative is to use somewhat lighter tackle and jig for the fish. Several 100 lb (45.3 kg) halibut have been caught on pirk-type baits. Other fast heavy fish, suspected of being big halibut, have been hooked fairly frequently on jig baits but have always managed to smash the rod, reel or line before being brought to the surface. A shoulder harness and rod-butt rest of the groin-protector type are essential. The halibut is the great challenge to British sea anglers: it fights its weight and, so far, little or nothing is really known of its movements.

83

Ling

Although ling have elongated eel-like bodies, they are members of the cod family. Ling are easy to distinguish from conger on account of their long bodies, broad heads and wide tooth-filled mouths. They have two dorsal fins and a single long barbule under the chin. Ling vary in colour from one area to the next, but are usually grey or greeny-brown in colour. In some, the body is mottled with darker spots and blotches; smaller ling seem prone to this effect. Ling, like conger, can grow to vast size, and specimens of over 700 lb (317 kg) have been taken by commercial methods. However, any angler fortunate enough to boat a ling of over 25 lb (11.3 kg) can be proud of his catch; although ling in excess of 50 lb (22.6 kg) have been taken on rod and line.

As a fighting species, ling are a better proposition than conger. Most of the ling I have caught made several long runs before rolling up to the gaff. A 35 lb fish (15.8 kg), which I hooked while fishing a mark south-east of the Lizard in Cornwall, fought extremely hard. I was convinced at the time that I had hooked a good-sized tope, for the ling's fast erratic runs were very similar to the fight pattern of a tope. Ling, like conger, are lovers of wrecks and sunken rocks. Unlike conger, however, ling often feed well up off the bottom. Large ling can occasionally be encountered over flat ground and I have had several 20 lb (9 kg) or more specimens while drifting over sandy ground in this way. Ling catches in excess of 5,000 lb (2,265 kg) have been made in recent years, mostly by West Country wrecking boats. At one time ling stocks were thought to be confined to West Country, Irish and Scottish marks. Evidence now shows that ling are more widespread than was first supposed; with south-coast charter boats finding concentrations of ling as far east as the straits of Dover. Wrecking has produced very large ling, off Yorkshire, from areas where such fish have been unknown.

Ling are greedy fish. Once they have been induced to feed, sport can be assured. Unlike conger, which tend to be cautious feeders, a big ling is a voracious biter, which pulls the rod tip hard down as it engulfs the bait. Ling are predators and can be caught on all types of squid and fish bait. On the famous Foghorn mark, off Fowey, I have hooked some very good ling on live pouting baits. On wrecks, however, I have always found fresh mackerel-fillets to be the most successful lure. Ling fall easily to baited pirk lures. The bigger the bait, the better it seems to work. West Country wreck anglers use huge pirk baits, baited with whole or filleted mackerel. These vast baits have proved highly attractive to large ling. One wreck-boat skipper swears that ling up to 100 lb (45.3 kg) in weight exist on many wrecks. In his opinion, most anglers use too small a bait to interest large ling. I agree with this theory. A 50 lb (22.6 kg) or more ling is a big fish with an appetite to match. A mackerel-strip bait can hardly be expected to interest such a giant. Most anglers forget that ling live in a food-rich environment. Wreck marks are alive with pouting, sea bream and medium-sized pollack, so resident ling packs find food easy to come by, and become preoccupied with fish well above the size of bait used by most anglers. Think big, use big baits and you will catch big ling.

Tackle

Ling are hard fighters, and robust tackle is essential for ling fishing. Use light conger tackle; anything much lighter could lose you an exceptional fish. Big ling, hooked close to some obstruction, invariably make a dive for home the moment they feel the hook. This initial power dive can be very difficult to stop, but stop it you must, for once the ling gets its head down into cover, a breakage is inevitable. Ling often make long runs against heavy rod pressure, and although they do not fight as long as conger of similar size, they are more of a sport fish than eel. Unfortunately, ling have a tendency to blow out when hooked as fish hooked in deep water often become air-filled due to the pressure change: the swim bladder usually extending from the mouth of the fish. Bloated fish seldom fight for long.

Usually, they float up and, even if lost on the surface, continue to float until gaffed.

There was a time when I thought that Scottish waters would produce some very big ling. Now I am not so sure. As yet, only a few Scottish sea-fishing grounds have been exploited, although some very good ling catches have been reported. These indicate high stocks of this species off the Scottish coast. Unfortunately, to date, Scottish ling over 20 lb (9 kg) have proved extremely elusive. Evidence suggests that, although prolific, Scottish ling seldom attain the weight achieved by southern ling. Interestingly enough, ling, like several other species, appear to be moving into areas where they were previously unrecorded. Off the Isle of Wight, for example, medium-weight ling are now reasonably common and, hopefully, stocks will become established enough to provide good sport for local anglers.

Mackerel and Garfish

Every sea angler must be familiar with the mackerel, for vast shoals of these handsome fish can be found all round the British Isles during the summer season. Mackerel are predators, feeding on the fry of herring, sprat and pilchard, and on sand eels. During the spring mackerel feed on the great banks of drifting plankton, but at all other times they are fish eaters. Mackerel grow to well over 4 lb (1.8 kg) but most rod-caught specimens weigh 1-2 lb (0.45-0.9 kg). Without doubt, on a weight-to-weight ratio, mackerel are the gamest fish any angler could wish to catch. Another hard-fighting fish to be found in company with mackerel shoals is the garfish. Anglers seeing a garfish for the first time often assume that it is some form of small swordfish, as its elongated body and bird-like beak give it the appearance of being a member of the swordfish family. If garfish grew to a respectable size, they would probably be the most sought-after species on the British list. Once a garfish feels the hook it's fireworks all the way. A hooked garfish puts on a spectacular display of acrobatics and spends as much time out of the water as in it. One of its favourite tricks is to stand on its tail and skitter across the surface for several yards before cartwheeling back into the sea. I have seen a big garfish jump clean over the bow of the dinghy from which I was fishing. On light tackle any garfish, regardless of size, can be relied upon to put up a magnificent struggle before it is subdued.

Like mackerel, garfish have a wide distribution but are probably commonest along the southern and south-western coastline of the British Isles.

Contrary to popular belief, garfish make good eating. When cooked, their bones turn green. A colloquial name for this species is, in fact, 'greenbone'.

Garfish are essentially surface feeders, but during excessively bad weather, they will hunt for food at seabed level.

A very similar fish to the true garfish is the skipper or saury pike, which is of little or no real interest to the angler.

Methods

Spinning

Both species are active predators and spinning with small artificial baits is probably the best way of catching them. For this sort of fishing, a light 7 or 8 ft (2.1 or 2.4 m) hollow-glass spinning rod, fixed-spool reel and nylon line of 6 or 8 lb (2.7 or 3.6 kg) breaking strain, should be used. An outfit like this will give the fish a chance to show its fighting ability to the utmost. Neither species is fussy about lures. Anything shiny, which spins, wobbles or vibrates as it is being retrieved will bring instant response if mackerel or garfish are on the move. My favourite spinners for this sort of work, are bar spoons such as the Voblex or medium Mepps. Both work well and set up a vibration pattern that attracts fish. Mackerel are much easier to hook than garfish for, although both species hit a bait as hard as they can, the narrow, hard beak of the garfish does not give much purchase to the hook point. The big mouth of a mackerel, on the other hand, gives a secure hold every time. Few mackerel are lost in comparison with lost garfish. Both fish seem to be attracted to fast-moving baits. It is, therefore, best to retrieve at speed, and forget about working the bait up and down or from side to side to try to simulate wounded or sick fish.

Spinning with light tackle can be great fun and very rewarding. I recommend this method for the angler who wishes to catch plenty of mackerel and get some real sport at the same time.

Driftline fishing

When fishing alone or with one other angler from a small boat, pier or harbour, driftlining can be used to catch mackerel and garfish. Only the lightest of tackle should be used for this method; the best bait being a sliver of skin from the belly of a fresh mackerel or garfish. This cutting should be $\frac{1}{2}-\frac{3}{4}$ in (1.3-1.9 cm) wide and 4 in (10 cm) long. To work properly it should be hooked just once on a size 4 or size 6 hook (see Fig. 49). In operation, the tackle should be cast out and allowed to drift away with the tide. The rod should be held at all times and the line must be fed smoothly off the reel spool. Expert driftline fishermen often use a small free-running centre-pin reel for this form of fishing, as the pull of the tide, on bait and line, is usually sufficient to turn the reel drum. In this way the bait works along naturally at the same speed as the tide. Mackerel and garfish shoals can be kept on the feed by dropping an occasional handful of chopped-up fish scraps into the water.

(Fig. 49)

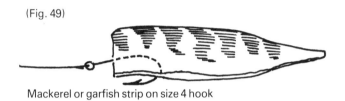

Mackerel or garfish strip on size 4 hook

Float fishing

When float fishing for mackerel or garfish, it is essential to decide at what depth the fish are feeding. Sometimes you will find that the shoals are harrying small fry right on the surface; more normally, you will be forced to find their feeding depth by a process of elimination. The only practical way to achieve this is to gradually increase the depth of the float-setting until bites are registered. In very shallow water, a fixed-float can be used (see Fig. 50), but when the depth of the water exceeds the length of your rod, a small streamlined sliding float must be employed (see Fig. 51). Where possible, the tackle should be cast out and allowed to drift with the tide for as long as possible. If a bite does not occur, the tackle should be slowly wound back and recast.

Never retrieve a bait at speed. Instead, work it back slowly in the hope that a hungry fish will be attracted by its flash. To give additional movement to the bait, stop your tackle at regular intervals so that the force of the current can sweep the bait to the surface (see Fig. 52). This movement often catches fish.

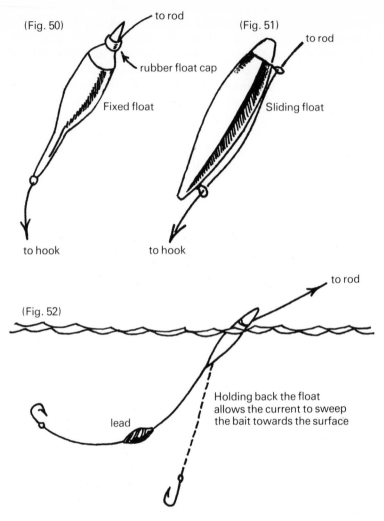

(Fig. 50)

to rod

rubber float cap

Fixed float

(Fig. 51)

to rod

Sliding float

to hook

to hook

to rod

(Fig. 52)

Holding back the float
allows the current to sweep
the bait towards the surface

lead

A long rod is best for float fishing. When a bait is a long way
out a short rod will not have the necessary leverage to pick up
the line and set a hook. My own choice of rod for this sort of
fishing is a 10 ft (3 m) hollow-glass carp rod, which I use with a
medium-sized fixed-spool reel.

The size of float depends, of course, on conditions. In any
event, sea floats should be kept as small and as streamlined as
possible. Many anglers use bulky floats, without considering
that fish such as mackerel are too small to pull a big float right

under, and will, in all probability, spit the bait out as soon as they feel the weight of the float. Fortunately, tackle manufacturers have now started to produce some good medium-sized floats.

Some years ago I developed a self-striking float for catching mackerel and garfish, and found that, at extreme ranges, it hooked the bulk of the fish that took the bait. This float is only suitable for fast-biting fish such as mackerel, but it is a useful addition to the tackle box and is well worth making up at home. The basic float body is constructed from 1 sq in (6.45 sq cm) balsa blocks, drilled out to take a thin plastic tube. Between the first and second block, a perspex disc, twice the diameter of the balsa, should be fitted and glued firmly into place. The body of the float can then be shaped, rounded off, waterproofed and painted ready for use. In action, the disc sits on the surface of the water and the moment a fish snatches at the bait and dives, the pressure of the water against the perspex plate drives home the hook. This float is useful for long-range work against shy biting fish.

The only practical weight to use with float tackle is a barrel lead, and a mackerel float should only be large enough to support a $\frac{1}{2}$ oz (0.014 kg) lead. If it needs more weight to cock it, it is far too heavy for this sort of fishing.

Feathering for mackerel

To my mind, catching mackerel six at a time on strings of feathers is not a sporting way of taking fish, although when I require a quantity of fresh mackerel for bait I automatically use these lures. I never cease to be amazed at the way most anglers are content to haul out string after string of fish on feathers. They cannot possibly hope to eat or give away the fish and yet, knowing full well that the bulk of their catch will go to waste, they continue to fill up every container on the boat and talk in terms of hundreds of fish in a single day. Competition men are a little more sporting, and most clubs fish to a three-feather only rule. There is no skill in catching mackerel on feathers. Once a large shoal is located, the fish hang themselves on the feathers until either the shoal disappears or it is time for the anglers to pack up and go home.

Most anglers buy their strings of feathers already made-up, from their local tackle dealer. Shop-bought feathers are usually dyed a variety of bright colours, but plain-white hackle feathers taken from the neck of an ordinary chicken are just as deadly. Half an hour spent at home, whipping a few long hackles on to sea hooks will save a lot of money, for commercially-tied feathers are not cheap.

The technique of feathering is simple. A string of feathers is tied to the reel line and a lead is tied to a length of line below the last feather (see Fig. 53). The whole rig is then lowered over the side, to the depth at which the fish are feeding. Then, by raising and lowering the rod tip, the feathers are jigged up and down in the water until a series of 'knocks' indicate that the mackerel are hanging themselves on the hooks.

(Fig. 53)

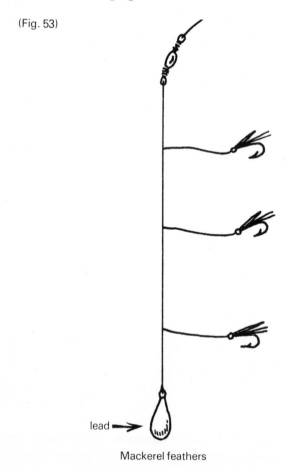

lead ➤

Mackerel feathers

My advice to any angler wishing to catch mackerel on feathers is to take a leaf out of the competition-anglers book and limit his gear to three feathers only. A self-imposed limit of this kind will practically eliminate the danger of a loose hook snagging some other person in the boat. Not only do I believe that there should be a strict limit on the number of feathers used, I also believe that a definite limit should be imposed on the quantity of mackerel any one angler can catch and kill in a day's fishing. There is no possible method of enforcing a rule of this kind. But if each angler retained only the fish he could use (or give away), it might well cut down the terrible and totally wasteful slaughter that takes place each summer.

The freshwater angler can, of course, use a trout-fly rod and reservoir lure to catch fish. This is an exciting form of fishing, well worth a little of anyone's time, but it is only really practicable when one is fishing alone in a small boat.

Mullet

There are four types of mullet in British waters; three kinds of grey mullet; and the small red mullet, which is very rare and of little interest to sport fishermen. The three kinds of grey mullet are: the thin lipped; the thick lipped; and the golden-grey mullet, the latter being identified by its golden cheek patches. Average mullet weigh $1\frac{1}{2}$-3 lb (0.7-1.4 kg). Anything above 5 lb (2.3 kg) is a good catch and anything over 6 lb (2.7 kg) a specimen. I have had several mullet over this weight, all taken from West Country estuaries, as well as a great many mullet of 4 lb-5 lb (1.8-2.3 kg). Mullet are shoal fish, with the largest shoals comprised of the smaller specimens. The big fish are, as a general rule, found only in small groups; because of this, it is very difficult to catch more than one or two big mullet at a sitting. With the medium-sized fish, catches of up to a dozen are common enough and, even on a bad day, it is usually possible to catch enough fish to feed an average family. Mullet are a southern species. They are common from the Essex coast round to Land's End, they are also common round the Channel Islands and the south-west coast of Ireland. Channel Island rock marks have produced a good many large mullet over the years but, for extra-big fish, the Portland marks are still the best place to fish. There are many marks in Cornwall and Wales which produce good catches of prime mullet. Some huge mullet, to over 14 lb (6.3 kg) have been taken in recent seasons. These giant specimens have all been taken near the warm water outlets of power stations, and there can be little doubt that constantly high sea temperatures cause rapid growth in mullet.

In the natural state, mullet feed mainly on algae and soft mud, from which they extract minute aquatic organisms. Mullet which regularly feed on weed usually make poor table

94

fish, as their flesh tastes strongly of weed and mud. Mullet can be classed as scavengers, for they are quite happy to suck up almost any edible matter that comes their way. Because of this, mullet can be conditioned to take new baits and a few handfuls of groundbait will soon attract the mullet shoals.

Conservation of mullet

Mullet are shoal fish, and where you find one you will find dozens. It is rarely possible to catch mullet in quantity which, happily, makes it difficult to deplete the shoals in any one area. At the same time, however, many successful mullet anglers kill all of the fish they catch, irrespective of whether they can use them. This is wrong, for a good many sporting fish are destroyed unnecessarily, and indiscriminate killing of this sort must be stopped.

We are living in an age when fish are being caught in vast numbers by commercial fishermen and in a world where industrial pollution is rife. Shoaling mullet are particularly susceptible to both these dangers, for they can be netted in huge numbers and, worse still, have a tendency to feed in rivermouths and harbours where polluted water often takes a deadly toll. Needless to say, most thoughtful anglers are well aware of these problems; but many do not seem to realise that, by returning a percentage of their catch, alive and unharmed, to the water they are safeguarding their sport in future years. There is also a great deal of satisfaction to be gained from returning a fish to its natural element.

The largest catch of mullet I ever made was 35 fish at a single tide. These weighed 3 lb–5 lb (1.4–2.3 kg) each. Collectively, my catch was extremely heavy but out of this huge catch I retained only four fish, which totalled over 12 lb (5.4 kg) in weight. The remainder of this catch were put back into the sea as they were caught. Freshwater anglers have learned the value of conservation and sea anglers must now follow, because it will not be long before many of our fish start to become scarce, and the sooner all anglers realise they can help preserve these fish the better things will be. Shoaling mullet are very easy to foul hook and, in a good many places, so-called anglers make a regular practice of snagging mullet on a weighted trace carrying two or three large treble hooks. Many of the fish foul-hooked

95

in this manner manage to tear free from the hooks and are left to die with gaping wounds in backs, sides or bellies. I am afraid to say that this practice is on the increase.

Tackle

Mullet fishing is very specialised and there can be no question of using standard sea-fishing tackle when mullet are the target. To justify the expense of an outfit that can only be used to catch one type of fish calls for a lot of thought, and the angler who decides to purchase such an outfit should be prepared to put it to good use at every possible opportunity. Fortunately, mullet fishing is one branch of angling which quickly becomes an obsession and most mullet anglers tend to become rather fanatical about it. This is understandable, for mullet are, even at best, a difficult species to catch and the challenge they present to the average angler is so great that the angler looks upon each mullet as a great personal achievement. Someone who has not experienced the frustrations of mullet fishing may find this hard to understand, but mullet fishing is completely different to all other forms of angling and the person who gains enough knowledge to take mullet consistently is a real angler. Great patience, skill and angling knowledge is essential if you want to catch mullet.

The most frustrating thing about grey mullet is the way it shoals in large numbers and shows itself readily to the angler and at the same time refuses to take the slightest notice of baited tackle. This behaviour is more than enough to drive many anglers away, to less difficult fish. There are occasions, of course, when a mullet shoal will go food-mad and will bite wildly, even at baits presented on tackle. This is a rare occurrence and, as a general rule, only the lightest of gear should be used. Even with ultra-light tackle, a good many fish will manage to shake free of the hook. The mouth of a mullet is very soft and tears easily under pressure. I have tried to overcome this unfortunate problem but I have still to find any true solution. Like most mullet fishermen, I have resigned myself to losing a fair percentage of the mullet I hook. Mullet fight as well as bass of similar size. Consequently, breakages also occur and I would say that any angler who lands one out of every three mullet hooked has reason to feel satisfied.

When selecting an outfit for mullet fishing, bear all these things in mind and go to a tackle shop which stocks freshwater gear, for it is among this type of tackle you will find the ideal mullet-fishing rod, reel and line.

Rods

Many cheap glass spinning rods have found their way into British tackle shops in recent years. A good many mullet enthusiasts have wasted money on these rods, for although they are cheap, and are quite serviceable for mackerel-spinning from boats, they are too short and too stiff for mullet fishing. This type of rod is seldom more than 7 ft (2.1 m) long and, in my experience, the minimum length of a mullet rod should be 10 ft (3 m). Remember that it is almost impossible to cast float tackle accurately with a short rod, nor is it possible to strike properly at a taking fish or, for that matter, to control a hooked fish correctly. These problems do not occur with a long rod, and although a long rod costs more than a short rod it is worth the additional expense. The ideal rod is a two or three piece hollow-glass trotting rod of the type used by Thames and Avon anglers. These rods are designed to cast and control light float tackle easily, and yet still have the backbone to play out a really big fish under difficult conditions. Remember that these rods are made for freshwater use, and the fittings are not anodised to protect them from the corrosive action of salt water or salt spray, so always wash it thoroughly with fresh water after each trip and then wipe it over with a soft rag soaked in machine oil. This will stop the rings and fittings rusting out in a few months: replacing them can be a costly job, even if you do it yourself.

Reels

For close range fishing, a freshwater centre-pin with a freely revolving drum is a pleasure to use. I use an Avon Royal Supreme. For long range fishing and general use a medium-sized fixed-spool reel is the best type. The slipping clutch mechanism of this kind of reel is invaluable for mullet fishing. Provided that this clutch is set correctly, so that the reel-spool will turn under the pull of a running fish, the problem of smashed tackle can be minimised. This problem can never be completely eliminated, for a big mullet takes off at high speed the second it feels the hook strike home. The resulting jerk can easily break

97

a light line. I set my clutch well below the breaking strain of the reel line; this gives me a better chance of avoiding a breakage in the initial stages of the fight. As the hooked fish weakens, I gradually tighten the clutch so that I can bring the fish into the waiting net. Once the fish has been landed, unhooked and disposed of, the next job is to re-adjust the clutch so that it can slip under the pressure of the next mullet. Never crank the reel handle while a fish is making the spool revolve. This twists and kinks the line, and may weaken it to such an extent that it will snap under a little strain. By all means hold the reel handle, but never turn it while the reel spool is slipping under clutch pressure. Reels should be cleaned after each outing, for salt water is dangerous to unprotected metal, and sand has a habit of getting inside the reel.

Lines

A monofilament line of 4 lb (1.8 kg) breaking strain should be used for all forms of mullet fishing. This may sound light for sea fishing, but remember that mullet of all sizes are quick to notice a thick line, and that the ideal mullet rod is designed to handle lines of this breaking strain. Almost any well known make of line will suffice, and most manufacturers give a wide choice of line colours in each individual breaking strain. One of the first things I do, whenever I float-fish for mullet, is to thoroughly grease the line so that it floats on the surface. This makes for faster and easier striking, although a floating line can be more difficult to control than a sunken one, particularly on windy days when the line has a tendency to 'bag' and drag the float away from the right area. However, this is a minor problem and a floating line is, in my opinion, essential for most forms of mullet fishing. Most tackle shops stock a good brand of line grease and a single tin should last two or three seasons.

Hooks

Even the fussiest angler should be able to find a hook which suits his mullet fishing. Remember that sea hooks are too large and too thick in the wire for mullet fishing, but that there are plenty of freshwater hooks which suit this form of fishing. Personally, I like to use a 12 or 14 eyed-hook in gold or bronze finish.

Floats

I consider a selection of floats to be an essential part of mullet fishing equipment. None of the floats I carry are designed for sea fishing, and many are simply bird or porcupine quills. Like all the other terminal equipment, floats should be kept as small and as streamlined as possible. For close range work, two-shot or three-shot quills are ideal while, for long range fishing, I find a slim cork or balsa-bodied trotting float (see Fig. 54) more useful. These floats should be attached at both ends, by means of two rubber float caps. In this way, if a change of float is called for, it is a simple operation to substitute one float for another without breaking down all the terminal tackle.

(Fig. 54)

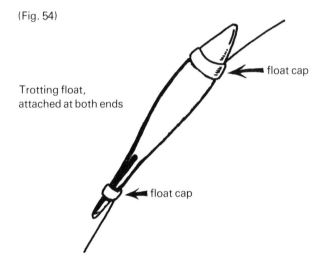

Trotting float,
attached at both ends

float cap

float cap

Additional tackle

A box or two of BB split shot, and a dozen very small barrel swivels, should always be carried. A coil of fine lead wire is also useful. For paternostering, a selection of pear-shaped leads, ranging from $\frac{1}{4}-\frac{3}{4}$ oz (0.007–0.02 kg) should be carried. Always make sure that you have plenty of leads, swivels and hooks. For they are easy to lose, and unless you have enough to carry on with, you might find that you have to stop fishing because of one small item of equipment.

99

A standard landing net is the best implement to use for landing mullet. Under normal circumstances, one with an ordinary 4 ft (1.2 m) handle would be sufficient but, when fishing from high rocks, an extendible handle can be an asset: these give an over-all length of 8 ft (2.4 m), which should be long enough to over-come most landing problems. Take great care, however, to ensure that the locking joint on the net handle is kept clean, well oiled and free from corrosion.

Times

To be successful, the mullet angler must be prepared to get up well before dawn, and start fishing at first sign of light. Obviously, the state of the tide must be taken into account. The ideal circumstances for mullet fishing are when first light coincides with a rising tide. Unfortunately, this only occurs a few times each season but, providing there is enough water to cover the bottom, the mullet will come nosing in as the sun starts to rise. If the area has been thoroughly groundbaited beforehand, then sport can be expected straight away. If not, then the mullet should be encouraged to feed by liberal use of groundbait. I have caught mullet at all times of the day, but my best results have always been obtained during the first few hours of daylight. As yet, I have never caught mullet after dark, although I have sometimes stayed on after a good day's fishing in hope of further sport. I do not know why mullet do not take hook baits once darkness has fallen, for they are often active at night and in my commercial fishing days I regularly took mullet in nets during the night.

Baits

Mullet are a soft-mouthed sucking fish; quick to accept new types of food, they always suck rather than bite at a bait, and their natural inclination is towards soft foods. There are many baits that can be used to catch mullet, some of which require special preparation.

Bread, in one form or another, has accounted for many of the largest mullet yet caught in the British Isles. Because of this, bread can rightly be regarded as a top bait, and one which every mullet angler should experiment with. The simplest, and easiest type of bread bait to use, is flake. Flake is the name given to the moist inside of a new loaf. To bait a hook with flake, a portion of bread, the size of a thumbnail, should be pinched from the inside of the loaf then folded round the shank of the hook. Only the bread round the shank of the hook should be squeezed, so that the portion covering the bend and point of the hook remains ragged and soft (see Fig. 55). This is important, for if the whole bait is compressed it will harden in the water and mar the penetration of the hook when the strike is made. Flake is comparatively heavy and can be cast well on floatless leadless tackle. Once in the water, it sinks slowly and naturally and is most attractive to mullet.

(Fig. 55)

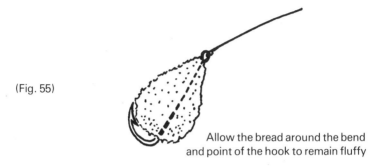

Allow the bread around the bend and point of the hook to remain fluffy

Very occasionally, mullet can be induced to feed on the surface. When this occurs, breadcrust can be a deadly bait. The best crust comes from a day-old tinned loaf. Some anglers cut their crust baits into neat cubes, but I prefer to tear my baits from the loaf, so that each separate bait appears as natural as possible to the feeding fish. A piece of crust the size of a penny can be used when big mullet are known to be in the area, but for medium-sized fish, a piece the size of a halfpenny will suffice. In its natural dry state, crust is too light a bait to cast any distance but weight can be gained by gently dunking the crust in the water before making your cast.

Bread paste is a first-class bait for mullet and one which has brought me a great deal of success. Many anglers have difficulty in making good bread paste, for it takes experience to make a paste that is neither too hard or too soft. The best paste is made from the flake of a day-old loaf. Tinned loaves are best because it is easy to remove all trace of crust from these. This is important, for I find that paste which contains crust quickly breaks up when immersed in water.

Having prepared the bread by removing the crust, the next step is to break the flake of the loaf into two equal parts. Soak the first part in fresh water until it is thoroughly saturated, then work it through your fingers to get rid of any excess water. Now using the second part, gradually knead the dry bread in with the wet bread. This mixture must be worked until a smooth paste is achieved. This should be strong enough to adhere to the hook during casting but soft enough to pull off the hook when the strike is made.

Having made enough paste for a day's fishing, wrap it in a clean white cloth, so that it can be transported without drying out or picking up dirt en route. Plain bread paste can be flavoured or coloured to personal choice; the addition of a little custard powder, for example, turns the paste yellow; while honey, cheese, fish paste and pilchard oil give the bait a distinctive flavour. I know anglers who go to extreme lengths to add to the attractiveness of their paste but, although I have used coloured and flavoured paste on many occasions, I have never found it to be any better or, for that matter, any worse than plain bread and water paste. If, however, you feel more confident using a specially prepared paste, then use it by all means, for confidence in your bait is, without doubt, nine-tenths of the battle.

On several occasions I have caught good-sized mullet while using cubes of soft cheddar or processed cheese. Cheddar seems to be a better fish catcher than processed cheese but both have taken their fair share of fish, and a flat box of processed cheese is easy to carry and keep fresh, and it makes a good standby bait.

I first started using raw meat to catch mullet while fishing at a spot where a pipe from a local abattoir emptied directly into the sea. I later experimented at other venues and found that raw meat made a good general bait. Minced meat can be bought from most butcher's shops and 1 lb (0.45 kg) of this will be more than enough for a day's fishing.

Another soft bait mullet seem to like is banana. I can give no explanation for this, and can only presume that it is the combination of colour, smell and softness that attracts mullet to a banana-baited hook. Baiting up with banana can be a little tricky at first. Banana is very soft and the strike should be made at the slightest sign of a bite, otherwise mullet will quickly suck the hook clean.

Tiny harbour ragworm make good mullet bait. They are, however, rather messy to dig and use, for harbour mud is glue like and has an indescribable smell. Harbour rag are very soft, and break easily when being placed on a hook. Sections of large ragworms are ideal when used in conjunction with mullet spoons (see spinning section of this chapter).

Freshwater anglers use maggot baits to catch a wide variety of fish, and although I have not given these grubs an extensive trial as sea bait, I have used them on several occasions to catch average-sized mullet. Maggots can be bought from many tackle shops. As baits they can be used singly or in twos or threes. They should be hooked through the skin on the square end of their bodies. This ensures that they stay lively and leaves the point and barb of the hook free to catch in the mouth of any mullet which takes the bait. It pays to throw the occasional handful of loose grubs into the water as groundbait if maggots are used as bait. Maggots are best fished on float tackle.

Small cubes of fish flesh make excellent mullet bait, particularly in areas where fish offal is dumped in quantity. Oily-fleshed fish, such as herring or mackerel, make the best baits. Care should be taken with fish baits, for mullet are very fussy and I have found that they will ignore any fish bait that has the slightest vestige of skin adhering to it. Flesh taken straight from a dead fish is often too soft to use right away. To overcome this problem, bait-sized sections of flesh should be cut, then left to dry in the sun for an hour or so before use.

During the late 1960s, I carried out a series of experiments with baits I had never tried before. One bait which proved to be highly successful was macaroni. In its ordinary uncooked state macaroni is of no use whatsoever but boil it for a few minutes in sugar-sweetened water and it becomes a clean, easy to use, and very deadly bait indeed. Small sections, about 1 in (2.5 cm) long are just about right. Use them on a size 14 hook and float tackle.

Peas were another bait which proved to be successful, and although I cannot say that I would prefer peas to other baits, I have proved to my own satisfaction that they are useful. They should be cooked as though for table use. This makes them soft enough to appeal to mullet and tough enough to stay on the hook during casting. Tinned sweet corn is another excellent mullet bait.

Successful mullet specialists use large quantities of groundbait to attract and hold the attention of the mullet shoals. Mullet are quick to discover groundbait and always seem prepared to sample any food scraps which come their way. A prime example of this is the way harbour mullet quickly learn to feed on bread scraps, most of which are the remains of holiday makers' picnic lunches, casually thrown into the harbour as food for gulls. Quite recently I watched a shoal of grey mullet jostling each other in a West Country harbour. The cause of their excitement was a handful of loose breadcrust which a visitor had just thrown into the water. Harbour mullet have ample opportunity to grow accustomed to unlimited free food, but the mullet shoals that live and feed round the average rock mark have to be carefully conditioned before they come to groundbaited areas; and even when they do arrive at such a place, they are quick to show fear at any sign of danger or rapid movement. This is understandable, for the mullet shoals that live and feed in isolated areas are not used to seeing human beings, whereas the harbour mullet soon become accustomed to the constant movement of a holiday crowd.

There are a great many ways of using groundbait to attract mullet; one of the best being to prebait a gully at the bottom of the tide, so that, as the water rises, a constant stream of groundbait is washed out to attract the fish. To prebait a gully in this way, I use a thick mixture of bran, chopped fish flesh and pilchard oil. This paste should be rammed into rock crevices on

(Fig. 56)

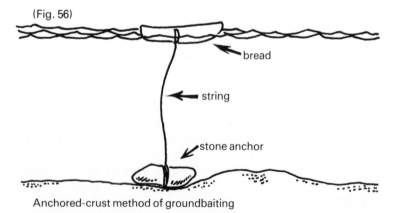

Anchored-crust method of groundbaiting

both sides of the gully. I do this in stages, starting at the low-water line and finishing at the high-water mark. In this way, the rising tide is constantly washing out a stream of food particles. By doing this correctly, mullet can be held right up until the slack period at the top of the tide; a time when I find mullet have a tendency to stop biting and disappear. I often use 10 or 12 lb (4.5 or 5.4 kg) of groundbait when prebaiting a gully in this way, as I feel it is better to overdo it rather than skimp on groundbait when mullet are the quarry.

The anchored-crust method of groundbaiting is useful for fishing in shallowish water (see Fig. 56). Once mullet learn that bread is good to eat, they often become preoccupied with it, and it can be a heart-stopping sight to see a shoal of very big mullet mouthing hungrily at a floating crust.

Methods

Float fishing

This is a highly effective method of catching mullet. A mullet outfit is extremely light by sea-fishing standards, and many anglers, who are used to heavy rods and large sea floats, find it difficult to adapt to the use of the river-type tackle necessary for all types of mullet fishing. This is understandable, for once a person is accustomed to casting floats which take anything up to 1 oz (0.028 kg) of lead to cock, the delicate art of casting a tiny two-shot or three-shot float is difficult to master.

However, once used to the lightness and delicacy of the outfit, most anglers find accurate casting easy. Mullet continually change their feeding depths. One day they feed hard on the bottom; the next, they only look at bait presented on the surface; the next, only at mid water. With float tackle it is easy to adapt to these changes and although there are many ways of catching mullet, float fishing is still the best all-round method. Unless fish are feeding right on the bottom, it pays to bunch the shot directly under the float (see Fig. 57), so that the bait sinks by its own weight alone. I have always found that mullet respond well to a bait which drops naturally through the water in this way. Because of this I make many of my mullet floats self-cocking by wrapping a suitable length of lead wire round the base of each float (see Fig. 58). Bunched shot does the job just as well, but a float that has been properly weighted is easier to

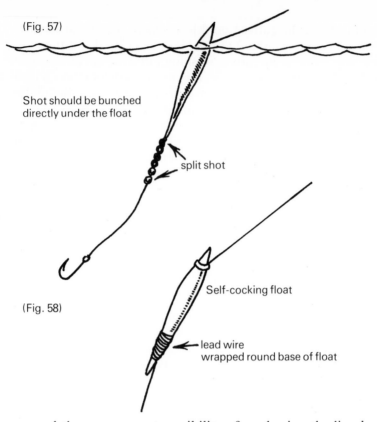

(Fig. 57)

Shot should be bunched
directly under the float

split shot

(Fig. 58)

Self-cocking float

lead wire
wrapped round base of float

use, and the ever-present possibility of weakening the line by pinching on split shot is eliminated. Of course, if the fish are feeding right on the bottom it will save time if your bait is made to sink as fast as possible. Under these circumstances, the shot can be placed some 6 in (15 cm) from the hook. In a normal sea, an ordinary quill or cork-on-quill float should suffice, but when the water is a little choppy then a long antenna float can be used to good advantage. These should be weighted so that just the tip protrudes above the surface (see Fig. 59). This type of float is amazingly steady in the water and will ride easily over rough seas.

Mullet bites vary a great deal, depending upon the depth at which the fish are feeding and on the shotting arrangement used to cock the float. When mullet are right on the bottom and the shot is close to the hook, a bite is usually registered as a sharp bob or as a savage pull which causes the float to disappear. With surface-feeding mullet, where the bait is allowed to fall through the water, the bite is normally indicated by the float tipping to one side before being dragged across the surface. No matter what kind of bite is given, your strike should be made the instant the float starts to move, for the bait will probably be soft and any delay in striking will give the mullet time to suck the hook clean and depart. To achieve even moderate success while float fishing requires good reflexes and a sharp eye. Even then, a good many bites will be missed completely, and even when fish are regularly being hooked the soft mouth of the mullet means that many will manage to shed the hook before being netted.

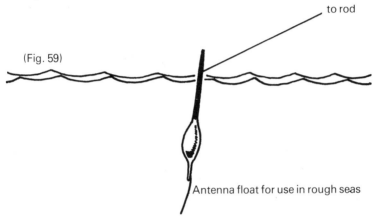

(Fig. 59)

to rod

Antenna float for use in rough seas

Surface fishing

In well-sheltered areas, where the water is little affected by wind or tide action, mullet shoals will often rise to the surface and laze in the sun. When this happens, they can seldom be induced to look at a bait presented on normal tackle; the only way I have managed to take fish under these conditions is by surface fishing. Breadcrust is the only bait which lends itself to this method and whenever I locate a shoal of basking mullet, my first thought is to scatter a few loose crusts on the water as groundbait. Mullet have an inbred curiosity which makes them inspect any edible-looking object which comes their way and although the first reaction of the shoal is to scatter in alarm when the crusts drop on the surface, they soon return to sample the bread. A shoal of mullet can clear a lot of groundbait in a remarkably short time, and once they begin to gulp down the loose crusts, the chances of catching a few fish are very high.

For surface fishing, no floats or weights of any kind are required; just rod, reel, line, hook and bait. Even a smallish piece of crust makes a fairly bulky bait. I use a size 8 or 10 hook for this form of fishing. Baiting up with crust requires practice, and the simplest method is to push the hook through the crust, turn it and push the hook point and barb through again (see Fig. 60). This will hold the bait firmly on the hook during casting and yet leave the hook point and barb masked so that when a fish takes the bait, the strike will set the hook into its lips. This is an exciting form of fishing for, having cast out the bait, every movement of the feeding fish is clearly seen and tension mounts as they approach the bait.

(Fig. 60)

Breadcrust baited on a size 8 or 10 hook for surface fishing

Generally speaking, there is little likelihood of catching a quantity of mullet on surface baits, for mullet are more wary than usual when they are close to the surface, and I normally find that after I have taken two or three fish, the shoal disperses for the rest of the day. Surface fishing is, without doubt, the most exciting form of mullet fishing. A few good fish taken in this way give me more pleasure than twice the number caught by other techniques and, whenever the opportunity occurs, I make a point of using the floating-crust method.

Using paternoster tackle

When mullet are bottom feeding in water too deep for comfortable float fishing, a light paternoster is the only practical form of terminal tackle. Most sea anglers use two-hook or three-hook paternoster rigs but I prefer to use one hook, particularly when mullet fishing, because two hooked-fish, both fighting for their lives can easily smash the ultra-light lines used for catching mullet. Even if they don't break the line, their combined strength will usually tear the hooks out of their mouths. For this reason I find a single-hook rig much better. All anglers have a tendency to use complicated terminal tackle, but for mullet which are line shy at the best of times, the simpler the gear the more it will catch. I make up my paternoster on the spot by sliding a tiny barrel swivel on to the reel line, stopping it some 12-15 in (30-38 cm) from the end of the line by means of a dust shot. Next, I tie a 9 in (22.5 cm) length of nylon line, with a 3 lb (1.4 kg) breaking strain, to the open eye of the swivel and attach a suitably-sized line to the open eye of the swivel and then attach a suitably-sized eyed-hook to the end of this trace. Finally, the whole rig is finished by a $\frac{1}{2}$ or $\frac{3}{4}$ oz (0.014 or 0.02 kg) weight, which is tied to the end of the reel line. This paternoster (see Fig. 61) is both simple and effective, and is ideal for deep-water work. Bread paste and fish flesh make the best baits for paternoster work. A paternoster is only effective if the line between rod tip and lead is kept as taut as possible, so that the bait is kept suspended just above the sea bed. To detect bites, a loop of line should be held in the left hand, while the rod tip should be carefully watched. The strike should be made at the slightest pull on the line or rod tip. Any delay will mean a missed fish and a lost bait. Paternostering is a very sensitive method and as there is a direct contact between rod tip and terminal tackle few bites should be missed on the strike.

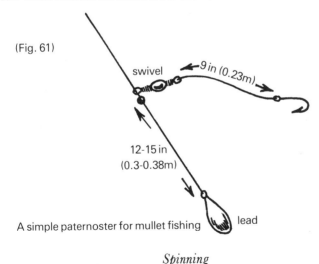

(Fig. 61)

swivel

9 in (0.23m)

12-15 in
(0.3-0.38m)

A simple paternoster for mullet fishing   lead

Spinning

Spinning for mullet is a comparatively new sport, which originated at Christchurch, in Dorset, where local anglers devised the method to catch shoaling mullet in the estuaries of the rivers Avon and Stour. Later this method moved westward to Plymouth and although, as yet, only a few anglers use this technique, it is a deadly style of fishing. Nowadays, mullet spoons can be purchased from most tackle shops. These are tiny bar spoons, mounted in the same way as a flounder spoon (see Fig. 62). The single hook, which trails behind the spoon blade, should be baited with a small ragworm or a section from the tail of a large ragworm. Mullet are not normally predatory but the sight of a baited spoon infuriates them to such an extent that they make a fast and savage attack on the bait. On those occasions I have used a baited mullet spoon, I have never returned home empty handed. Spoons with a touch of orange paint seem to be the most effective for mullet.

(Fig. 62)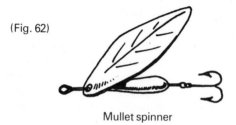

Mullet spinner

Pollack and Coalfish

Of all the medium-weight sea fish a boat angler is likely to encounter, pollack are among the gamest and most beautiful. They provide superb sport on light tackle, and on offshore grounds, particularly round reefs and wrecks, they grow to a large size. Pollack are an Atlantic species and the largest specimens invariably come from West Country waters. The waters off Devon and Cornwall are the best places in England for really large pollack but I have also had some fine specimens off the west coast of Scotland and off Orkney. I have caught many pollack off the Hampshire and Dorset coasts, but have never taken any of great size from this section of the Channel, although I strongly suspect that some real rod-benders lurk off the St Catherine's Lighthouse area of the Isle of Wight: fish up to 16 lb (7.2 kg) have been taken from this area recently.

Good-sized pollack are rarely to be found over sandy ground; the best pollack marks are invariably very rocky and tall under-water pinnacles and large sunken reefs are ideal. The Manacles, off South Cornwall, are a typical example of a good pollack mark, huge jagged rocks which sweep up to the surface from a considerable depth of water. In recent years, wreck fishing has accounted for huge pollack catches: most fish falling to artificial baits.

I find that pollack move from one ground to another throughout the season. In the early part of the summer, say May and June, they hug the pinnacles as closely as possible. Later, as the season progresses, they move further out and feed over rough and stony ground, within easy reach of the main rocky outcrops. In the late autumn, however, pollack become real wanderers and are likely to turn up almost anywhere. Big pollack are almost always found in deep water, whereas the smaller fish usually congregate on top of a reef or pinnacle. Because of this, it is best to fish at the base of any likely outcrop or wreck, rather than towards the top of it. I do not believe pollack to be true shoal fish, although they do congregate in vast numbers over likely feeding grounds. While fishing West Country marks, I have noticed that in late autumn and early winter big pollack often move inshore in large numbers. I have heard that this shoreward migration also occurs off the Irish coast but I have no personal experience of it. In Cornwall, the big fish come right in and are often caught by people float fishing or spinning from quays and rocks. At this time of year the small-boat angler, who cannot normally get out to the deep offshore pollack-grounds, stands a good chance of catching fine pollack over rough ground while remaining within easy reach of shelter should a storm brew.

Since wreck fishing began in earnest, the original pollack record has been smashed on numerous occasions. At one time a 16 lb (7.2 kg) pollack was regarded as a huge specimen. In recent years, however, a pollack has to weigh 20 lb (9.1 kg) or more to be regarded as a noteworthy fish. Hundreds of fish around this weight have been taken in recent years and, although commercial fishermen are now working many of the distant wreck marks, anglers are still bringing in huge catches.

The coalfish is very similar to the pollack in outward appearance. The easiest way of telling the two fish apart is by comparison of the lower jaw. If it projects well beyond the upper jaw, the fish is a pollack. If it recedes, or is the same length as the upper jaw, the fish is a coalfish. The lateral lines of the two fish also vary. The lateral line of the pollack is dark on a light background; while that of the coalfish is light on a dark background. Colour of both species varies considerably from one locality to another, with the brightest-coloured fish usually coming from fairly shallow water: these are a burnished-gold colour, with white or off-white bellies. Deep-water specimens are usually greyish-green with white underparts. Coalfish are, on average, rather darker than pollack, but light-coloured specimens occur in many areas. Pollack that are covered with dark flecks are also common – Cornish fishermen refer to them as 'teamakers'. Although big pollack or coalfish have quite a girth, they invariably have a long rakish appearance. Both fish are active hunters, capable of sudden bursts of terrific speed.

Coalfish have a wide distribution, are commonest in northern waters, and grow to a larger average size than pollack. The record for the species currently stands at 33 lb (14.9 kg) (larger fish have been caught by commercial fishermen). In Scottish waters, huge shoals of coalfish up to 5 lb (2.3 kg) in weight can often be encountered close to the shore. The larger specimens, however, seldom venture inshore of the 15–20 fathom line. My best catches have all been taken from deep offshore grounds during late autumn and early winter.

Coalfish can be encountered well away from rough ground, swimming at the midwater mark. I first found this out when I was feathering for mackerel over very deep water and hit a huge shoal of large coalies some 12 to 15 fathoms under the boat. At the time I hit these fish, the echo sounder was registering bottom at 30 fathoms. Stranger still was the fact that the sea bed was as flat as a pancake for some miles around without the slightest outcrop of rock showing above the mud and sand. Later, I took other catches of coalfish from similar areas. Pollack are usually much easier to locate than coalfish and, as a result, no techniques have been devised for catching coalfish. Most of those that are taken, fall to pollack-fishing methods.

Tackle

To take pollack and coalfish successfully throughout the season, it is necessary to use at least two separate sets of tackle. A light one for off-the-bottom work; and a heavier one for presenting a bait on or just off the sea bed or for trolling. My own light outfit consists of a hollow-glass 10 ft (3 m) carp rod and a small Penn multiplier. This outfit is capable of handling lines of up to 12 lb (5.4 kg) breaking strain, which I consider should be the maximum strength of line for off-the-bottom work.

For trolling or fishing on or just off the bottom, I use a 20 lb (9 kg) class boat rod, used in conjunction with 20 lb (9 kg) breaking-strain line and a 4-0 size multiplying reel. For wreck fishing, where snags abound, most anglers use a 30 lb (13.6 kg) class rod, and line to match. I stick to the lightest outfit I can, for a big pollack hooked on a long carp-type rod and comparatively light line provides all the thrills of big-game fishing at a fraction of the cost. It takes great skill to control the first wild power-dive of a good pollack with tackle of this calibre. A double-figure specimen can be relied upon to make run after run in its attempt to throw the hook.

Size 2-0 or 3-0 hooks should be used for general pollack fishing, but when extra-large fish are known to be in the area, the sizes should be increased to suit larger-than-average baits.

Methods

Trolling

Trolling should be used for fishing shallow inshore reefs, from a small boat powered by oars or a well-throttled-down outboard motor. I find that when I fish from a motor-driven boat the fish tend to stay well behind the boat, and can only be caught when there is a lot of line, say 60 yards/metres, streaming out astern. From a rowed boat, however, the opposite applies and the fish will often come to a lure trolled close behind the transom. Trolling a lure behind a boat has the advantage of showing the bait to fish scattered over a wide area.

Choice of bait depends on personal preference. Some anglers swear by a natural sand-eel bait for trolling, other equally-experienced and successful fishermen consider a rubber eel the deadliest of all trolling baits. The best rubber eels are the red-gill and the Eddystone eel, both of which are readily available from tackle shops. The beauty of these baits is their flexible tail, which gives the eel a natural swimming appearance in the water. In the old days, artificial eels were made out of stiff plastic tubing; this type of bait is still on sale but should be avoided. A stiff-tailed eel rotates and this unnatural action causes fish to shy away without striking at the bait.

One of the main drawbacks to trolling with rod and line is that while a lead must be used to hold the bait below the surface, the displacement of water behind the lead tends to put fish off. The only practical way of overcoming this is to set the lead far enough away from the bait for its disturbance not to matter. But this, in itself, leads to a problem. If a lead is set some 12 ft (3.6 m) away from the bait, and the angler uses, say, a 7 ft (2.1 m) rod, the lead will jam against the rod tip long before the fish can be brought within range of the gaff. Over the years, various quick release devices have been brought out to offset this problem but none of them can be relied upon to work on all occasions.

Personally, I use a simple valve-rubber stop, which folds up when wound hard against the top ring and so allows the lead to slide freely down the line so that the fish can be brought to the gaff. Under no circumstances should the lead be allowed to drop right down to the hook, however. If it does, it may hit the shank of the hook and knock it out of the fish's mouth.

Nowadays, I use a small swivel some 2 ft (0.6 m) from the hook, which acts as a secondary stop for the lead and helps eliminate any possibility of line kink should the bait start to twist in the water. Use a small swivel as large swivels often become clogged with weed and cease to function.

The amount of lead needed depends on the depth of water to be fished and on the time of day. Pollack, more so than coalfish, change their feeding level to suit the amount of light penetrating the water. For example, during the middle part of the day, when light intensity is at its highest, pollack stay as close to the bottom as possible. On dull days or in the late evening when light fades, they rise higher in the water and may be found at any level between midwater and the surface. I have had several pollack of over 12 lb (5.4 kg) on lures that were working only a couple of feet beneath the surface. These catches were all made at twilight, on calm sultry days, when light was low and sea and air temperatures were high.

Tide speed also affects feeding levels to some extent. At the full run of an ebb or flood tide, the fish often rise well off the bottom. By changing leads, and adjusting the speed of the boat to suit each changing stage of day and tide, it is possible to catch far more than an angler who is content to troll at one level on all occasions.

When fishing over shallow reefs, always make a wide arc when turning. A sharp turn will cause the line between boat and bait to fall slack, which sometimes allows the lure to snag up on the sea bed.

Live sand eels are a pollack bait second to none, and to fish them properly it is advisable to use light tackle at all times; the carp-type rod, small reel and light line being ideal for use with the live-eel baits. Only a light lead should be used. I find that a ½ or 1 oz (0.014 or 0.028 kg) spiral or barrel lead is usually sufficient to hold the bait down, particularly in West Country waters where tides are generally fairly slack. With a 10 ft (3 m) rod, I normally use an 8 or 9 ft (2.4 or 2.7 m) trace attached to the reel line by a small barrel swivel. The lead should set directly against this swivel.

I have already described the various ways of hooking a live sand eel in the Bass chapter. Any of these methods can be used for pollack fishing. With big eels, the best method to use is to slip the hook through the mouth of the eel and out of its gill slit. The point of the hook can then be snicked through the belly-skin of the eel. This gives a firm hold, which is essential, for big pollack are skilled at nipping a lightly-hooked bait off the hook. The size of the hook depends on the size of the bait. Large eels, for example, should be mounted on a size 3-0 or 4-0 hook.

Once the bait has been attached, the tackle should be lowered gently into the water and allowed to run out until the lead touches the bottom. Never drop the bait heavily into the water, as a sudden shock may well kill it. When the lead hits bottom, the tackle can be left as it is or slowly reeled up. Both methods catch fish, but when fish are in a finicky mood the moving bait is more likely to produce results.

Large pollack are often shy biters. The first time they snap at the bait they will barely move the rod tip. To strike at this first indication is a mistake. It pays to wait for the fish to really pull the rod tip over before setting the hook. The moment a good pollack is hooked, it will make a wild power dive towards the bottom. Because of this, the drag mechanism on the reel must be set lightly so that the fish can take line, otherwise a breakage will be inevitable. Newcomers to pollack fishing usually get smashed in this way a number of times before they learn to adjust their reel drag correctly. Unfortunately, the first burst of power from a hooked pollack is often its last. These fish burn themselves out very quickly indeed. There is a theory that the sudden change of water pressure, as the fish plunges into the depths, damages the swim bladder of the fish to such an extent that the fish is rendered incapable of continuing the fight; it is noticeable that large pollack hooked in shallow water usually fight longer and harder than fish of similar size taken from deep-water marks.

Once the taking depth is found, the fish will often stay at the same level for some time. In Cornwall, many anglers mark their line at the exact depth, by means of a bit of rubber band tied directly round the line. However, the feeding level may well change half a dozen times in a single day, so when fish stop biting at one level, work the tackle up and down until you make contact again.

In Scotland and, to a lesser extent, in Ireland, I have used a similar method to catch both pollack and large coalfish. Unfortunately, I have never been able to secure live sand eels in either country and have had to use long narrow fish strip as a substitute.

Using on-the-bottom tackle

I have caught many good pollack and coalfish while fishing with bottom tackle, from both anchored and drifting boat. Although I have caught good fish on legered baits, I much prefer to use a form of paternoster for this type of fishing, which I make up as follows: first, I tie a three-way swivel directly to the end of the reel line; second, I attach a 2 ft (0.6 m) length of 12 or 14 lb (5.4 or 6.3 kg) nylon to the middle eye of the swivel; and third, I fasten a 3 ft (0.9 m) length of similar line to the lower swivel eye and tie the lead to the loose end of it. The size of the weight depends on the speed of the tide. As a rough guide, the lead should be just heavy enough to hold bottom without rolling away. Bomb or pyramid leads are the best shapes to use for this type of fishing; bait can be a live sand eel or an elongated strip of fish skin. When fishing from an anchored boat, it is advisable to bounce the bait over the sea bed, by lifting and lowering the rod tip and releasing a yard/metre or two of line at regular intervals.

A natural bait can be made even more attractive by adding a revolving spinner, tied directly above the hook (see Fig. 63). In a strong tide the flow of water will cause this spinner to rotate, setting up both visual and vibratory waves which draw hunting fish to the bait.

(Fig. 63)

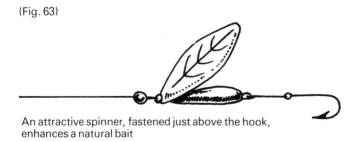

An attractive spinner, fastened just above the hook, enhances a natural bait

Float fishing (Shore)

For shore, pier or harbour waters, float fishing can be a killing technique. Live sand eels, elvers and prawns make the best bait for this form of angling; I am particularly fond of using large elvers as a float-fishing bait. They are both hardy enough to withstand the shock of being cast a considerable distance and highly attractive to predatory fish.

A 10 ft (3 m) carp rod is the ideal weapon for this form of fishing, and when it is necessary to make a long cast with light float tackle the rod should be used with a medium-sized fixed spool. Casting will often be unnecessary, as tackle can be dropped over the side of a boat and trotted out with the set of the tide. I like float fishing for pollack, and find that, more often than not, the float vanishes with a real bang. Bulky floats should not be used. These alarm a taking fish to such an extent that it drops a bait long before the hook can be struck home. In rough water, I sometimes use a round float, of the type used by pike anglers, as a pilot float. This can be bought in most good tackle shops for a fraction of the price of more elaborate floats, and converted into a serviceable sliding float for sea work by the addition of a short length of plastic tube. Although their round shape makes them appear more bulky than a long narrow float, they offer very little resistance to a biting fish and remain far more stable in rough water.

Driftline fishing

Although not widely used, the driftline technique can be used for both shore and boat fishing when fishing for pollack and coalfish. On slack tides, particularly during the late evening, I have used it successfully over deep-water marks but it lends itself best to fishing in moderate depths. A true driftline consists of rod, reel, line and hook. If additional weight must be used, it should be kept to the absolute minimum, otherwise it will interfere with the action of the bait in the water. I find that driftline tactics work best when used on the edge of a tidal current, of the type that often occurs just off a rocky headland. The technique is simple. The bait is dropped over the side of the boat, or cast out from the rocks, and allowed to drift with the flow of the tide. This is essentially a light-tackle method and although anglers should try to maintain fairly close contact with their bait, they should not check its natural movement in any way. Driftlining calls for a considerable amount of skill on the part of the angler. Many specialists dispense with the multiplier or fixed-spool reel in favour of a free-running centre pin. For driftline work, the centre pin, which should be kept grit-free and well oiled at all times, is the most sensitive of all reels. If a good well-balanced model is used, the pull of the tide on bait and line will be sufficient to turn the reel drum so that the bait runs out smoothly with the current.

Jigging

For the angler who prefers to use a single-hook rig, there are some excellent American jigging baits available (see Fig. 64).

(Fig. 64)

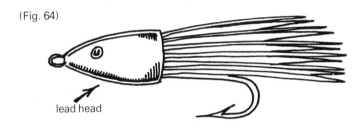

lead head

An American lead-head jig lure

Pirk-type lures can also be adapted. To cut costs many anglers make their own jig and pirk-style baits. I have made jigs from the door handles of an old car and from chromed tubes and all have caught big fish. Any angler should be able to knock up a selection of jig baits for practically nothing, provided that he is fairly handy with a set of tools. To increase the average life expectancy of the expensive commercially-made lures, it pays to attach the hook to the body of the lure by means of a length of line of lesser breaking strain than the reel line (see Fig. 65). Then, if the hook snags on the seabed, it should be possible to break the lure free losing only the hook in the process. Pollack and coalfish hit jig baits with a terriffic bang, so to get the utmost sport out of this type of fishing it pays to use lightish tackle. Choice of tackle, unfortunately, depends on strength of tide but, by using a wire line that cuts water resistance to a minimum, it is often possible to use 2–4 oz (0.056–0.11 kg) jig lures in strong tides.

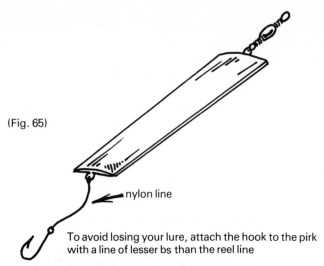

(Fig. 65)

nylon line

To avoid losing your lure, attach the hook to the pirk
with a line of lesser bs than the reel line

Wreck fishing has produced a great many big pollack, most
of which have fallen to baits which were worked or jigged over
the wreck itself. This is easy fishing; and the tackle is crude but
effective. Most anglers use a 12, 16, or 24 oz (0.34, 0.45 or
0.9 kg) pirk lure as a weight (see Fig. 66), with two rubber eels
fished on nylon fliers above the pirk. The trick is to drop the rig
until it touches the wreck, then work it up and down with
powerful sweeps of the rod, or else wind it up as fast as possible
until fish slam into one or all of the baits.
Not pretty fishing, but highly effective
for big fish. This method works for
both pollack and coalfish.

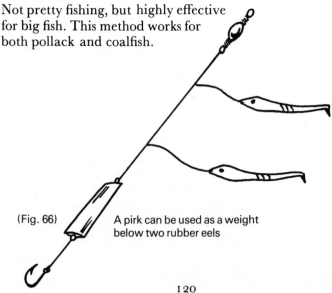

(Fig. 66)   A pirk can be used as a weight
below two rubber eels

Spinning

Spinning is a sporting way of catching both pollack and coal-fish, and is ideal for the angler who likes to keep on the move. One of the best places to catch pollack and coalfish on artificial lures is a weed-grown gully between two rocky reefs. In these places, the fish spend their time lurking amongst the thick bottom weed or patrolling along the submerged rock walls just above the weed beds. A spinner, or rubber eel, worked steadily along just above the weed or close to the rocks will usually produce rapid results. Light baits should be used when fishing under these circumstances, and these should be retrieved at a steady speed, so that they work at a set level, 1 ft (0.3 m) above the beds of sea weed (see Fig. 67). Any break in the rate of retrieve will result in the bait dropping into the weed where it will probably be snagged. To add a little extra life to the bait, the rod tip can be moved gently from side to side so that the bait zig-zags back through the water. At no time should the rate of retrieve be slowed down during this process.

(Fig. 67)

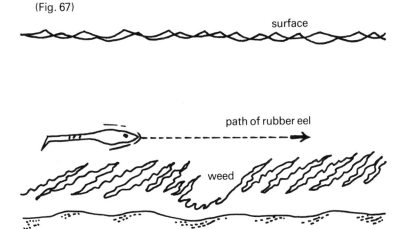

An artificial bait should be worked just above the weed line

A dozen casts in any one gully will show whether or not pollack or coalfish are present: if the bait isn't taken during these dozen casts, it is fairly safe to assume that no fish are about, and if this is the case, there is no point in wasting time. So the angler should move on to the next likely gully in search of fish. Both pollack and coalfish are shoalfish and where you catch one you should get more, so if a fish is caught it pays to work the bait through every fishable inch of the gully. It is possible to vary the rate of retrieve in deep water, so that the bait flutters and vibrates enticingly. Once again, the fish will spend most of their time close to the bottom so when fishing deeper-than-average water, larger heavier baits should be used. Obviously, the angler who keeps on the move will find himself fishing a deep gully one minute and a shallow one the next. Each will call for a change of lure so, to save time, it pays to tie a link swivel to the reel line so that lures can be clipped on and off in a moment. Never tie artificial lures directly to the reel line, for the lure will twist and kink the line to such an extent that the line will soon become unusable.

Skate and Ray

For years skates and rays have been classed under the general heading of either thornback ray or common skate. In other words, every small specimen has been regarded as a thornback, every big specimen as a common skate, irrespective of its species.

Fortunately, anglers are becoming increasingly record conscious, and most now take the trouble to learn to identify the various types of skate and ray. Club fishermen, on the other hand, still adopt a couldn't-care-less attitude and are content to bring fish to the scales to boost their end-of-season weight. To a large extent, club officials are the ones to blame for this lack of interest and knowledge, always bearing in mind that the organisation of a competition, and its subsequent end of day weigh-in, leaves little time for sorting out and identifying fish which are very similar in outward appearance. No doubt the day will come when each weigh-in will include a steward whose sole job will be to identify individual species as they are brought to the scales. To help clarify this situation there follows a detailed account of the types of skate and ray found around the shores of the British Isles. Knowing what fish you have caught adds to the overall pleasure of angling, and one day you may catch the record breaker. Many of the records on the British list are open; others are held by fish with very low weights, which should be easy to equal or beat if luck is on your side.

Thornback Ray

The thornback is one of the commonest of British rays and one of the most sought-after fish. As its name implies, it has a number of thorny spines on its back and tail. These can be very sharp and it is wise to handle a freshly-caught thornback very carefully to avoid injury. Most anglers carry an old piece of towelling, with which to pick up these spiky fish. The thornback is variable in colour; usually brown or greyish-brown on the back. This basic colour is overlaid, with pale spots surrounded by borders of small dark spots. Smallish fish have banded tails but these bands are often absent on large specimens. The underparts are white. Thornback grow to a comparatively large size and specimens of up to nearly 40 lb (18.2 kg) have been taken. The average run of rod-caught fish weighs 7–12 lb (3.2–5.4 kg). A 20 lb (9.1 kg) thornback being regarded as a good catch in most areas.

Thornback have a wide distribution and can be found in most places round the British Isles. They are plentiful in the English Channel; and some of the sea lochs in the Western Highlands of Scotland are thick with them. They are commonest where the seabed is comprised of sand, mud or gravel, though they can sometimes be caught over rocks. The skate grounds off the Isle of Wight are often a mixture of rock and flat clay mud, and these areas seem to produce larger-than-average thornback during most months of the year. They are generally regarded as a summer species, and they often feed in comparatively shallow water. In the winter they move offshore on to the deeper marks. Thornback, like all the skate and rays, are bottom feeders which live by eating crustacea, worms and small fish, which they catch or find dead. They tend to be scavengers and many of the successful thornback specialists swear by a stinking bait, and make a point of leaving herring or mackerel baits in the sun until smelly enough to attract a hunting thornback. Catches indicate that thornback usually travel in small groups, each group consisting of one female followed by several male fish. The female is usually the largest fish in the group. The female seems to be given first refusal of any food the group comes across, for, more often than not, it is the female that is caught first. Once the female has been caught, the male fish hang about under the boat and are often caught in quick succession. Very occasionally an exceptionally large group of ray will be encountered. I once found such a group, and my companion and I, had 22 ray between our two rods; this was an unusually large catch of fish, which I doubt if I will ever repeat.

Blonde Ray

During the past few seasons, several very large blonde ray have been caught by south coast anglers, as a result of which a new record for the species has been established. Unfortunately, a real record breaker of nearly 40 lb (18.2 kg) was eaten before its captor realised just what a monster he had boated.

The blonde ray is less angular than the thornback and lacks the large thornlike spines. The blonde is usually sandy-coloured on the back, with a thick sprinkling of small black spots which extend to the margins of the wings. There are also 9 or 10 pale roundels on the body disc. The underparts are white. Blonde ray grow, on average, to a larger size than thornback but are seldom caught in any quantity. They are common in the Channel and on the Atlantic coast, but seem to be rather rare in the North Sea. Most of the blonde ray I have caught or examined have been taken in fairly deep water. Hermit crab are a favourite food of the blonde ray, although most of the fish caught by rod-and-line anglers fall to fish-fillet baits of various types.

Homelyn or Spotted Ray

The spotted ray is often confused with the blonde ray for both fish have a similar basic appearance. However, the nose or snout of the spotted ray is more prominent than that of the blonde ray, and the overall colouring of the back is darker. The pale spots, although present on the back of the spotted ray, are less well-defined than on the blonde ray; although, on the few specimens I have seen, there has always been a single prominent pale blotch on each wing. In every case this has been bordered by a ring of small dark spots. Spotted ray are found all around the coast of the British Isles, generally in fairly shallow water. They are smaller than the blonde ray, but can be caught on large baits; though most of those I have caught or heard of, were taken on worm baits intended for plaice.

Cuckoo Ray

This fish is easy to identify. Its heart-shaped body and yellowish-brown back is most distinctive. To make identification even simpler, there is a large and dark eye-spot on each wing with yellow spots and wavy lines superimposed on it. Cuckoo ray have a wide distribution and, although by no means commonly caught, they have been recorded from most parts of the British coast. Most of the specimens taken have fallen to worm baits. Cuckoo ray are probably the smallest ray, and most of the fish I have examined weighed $1\frac{1}{2}$–3 lb (0.7–1.4 kg).

Painted Ray

The painted ray is also easy to identify, for its sandy-coloured back is covered with a series of dark lines and artistic blotches (the angling press nicknamed this fish the 'PopArt ray'). Painted ray seem to be common in the eastern half of the English Channel. Specimens have also been caught off South Devon, and south-west Ireland is a great place for this fish. Most specimens weigh 8–14 lb (3.6–6.3 kg). The painted ray is a scavenger like the thornback and can be caught on similar baits.

Small-eyed Ray

Ten years ago there was an influx of small-eyed ray into marks along the south coast of the British Isles. A number of fish of record-breaking size were taken and some large bags of average specimens were recorded. At first, many of the fish were mistaken for medium-sized blonde ray (which they closely resemble). Prior to this invasion, the only area from which I had caught small-eyed ray was a patch of mixed clay and rock off Freshwater Bay. Then, suddenly, the fish were everywhere – from the Straits of Dover down to Land's End – the Channel was alive with them.

The small-eyed ray is similar in shape to the blonde ray but is much paler in colour. All the specimens I have seen were a sandy colour on the back, with a series of pale spots and lines; the lines being most apparent on the extremities of the wings. The edges of the wings and the tail were outlined in brilliant white, giving the fish an overall neatness and clean-cut appearance.

Sting Ray

The sting ray is a localised fish which the vast majority of anglers will never have a chance to catch. The Solent and the Essex coast are the only places known to me where sting ray are at all common. Individual specimens have, however, been taken from many places in the Channel and can crop up at almost any point around the British Isles. Sting ray attain a good size, with a 20 lb (9.1 kg) fish being regarded as a small specimen. My best sting ray tipped the scales at 35 lb (15.8 kg); fish up to almost twice this weight have been caught! A Clacton angler, for example, caught a monster sting ray in 1952. This fish, although never weighed properly, was estimated to weigh around 70 lb (31.7 kg). In the Lymington area of the Solent, sting ray of around 40 lb (18.2 kg) are caught most seasons; and a trawler man working the Solent caught and released a monster ray thought to weigh 100 lb (45.3 kg). This huge fish was minus its whiplike tail, a sure sign that, at some time in its life, it had been caught by an angler, for in many areas beach anglers chop off a sting ray's tail before attempting to remove the hook. Sting ray are very similar in shape to skate, but they have a rounder overall outline. They are normally drab brown in colour with no spots or blotches; the underparts being a mottled white grey. The body of a sting ray is covered in a disgusting layer of thick, evil smelling slime.

The sting ray gets its name from its long whiplike tail, the jagged, bony spine of which can cause a very nasty wound. The tail spine is grooved and carries venom which can be intensely painful and can cause temporary paralysis. I know several anglers who have been cut by the thrashing tail of a big ray, and each has suffered very badly as a result. Sting ray are a summer species and the best months to try for them are June and July when they are found in shallow waters. It is generally believed that they migrate offshore during the winter months. However, I think they probably spend the winter months in hibernation in the thick mud of the Solent or the Essex creeks and marshes. Although I have known of sting ray taking fish baits, their favourite food is, without doubt, lugworm or ragworm, and any angler who wants to catch these fish will be well advised to use these worms as bait. Sting ray also feed on crabs and shellfish and I have hooked several on hermit-crab baits. I make a habit of returning all the sting ray I catch to the sea. They are messy fish to handle and there is little point in killing them. In spite of their ungainly shape and repulsive appearance, they provide good sport on reasonably light tackle, for they are powerful creatures, quite capable of short bursts of terrific speed.

Electric or Torpedo Ray

This is not a fish which the average boat angler is likely to see, let alone catch, but the odd specimen has been taken on rod and line and for this reason I feel it essential to include the fish. Like the sting ray, it can be an ugly customer to handle, and it is better to know what a particular fish is capable of doing before you actually try to touch it. Torpedo ray are easy to identify. They have a distinctive shape; the body disc being sub circular, cut off square across the front; the tail section being similar to, although stouter than, the tail of a monkfish. It has two dorsal fins, set close to each other near to the wrist of the tail, which resemble broad paddles and tend to sag to one side. The eyes and respiratory holes of the fish are very small and the skin is devoid of scales and very clammy to the touch. The back is slate grey with no extra markings. Torpedo ray are known to reach a length of over 5 ft (1.5 m) and a weight of over 100 lb (45.3 kg). An angler fishing off the quay at Mudeford, in Dorset, hooked a torpedo ray of over 60 lb (27.2 kg) which he eventually landed. A specimen I took on rod and line did not put up much of a fight and was easily brought to the boat. Torpedo ray live, for the most part, over soft bottoms where they feed on fish of all types. The torpedo fish is lazy and torpid, and catches its food by using the electric discharge from powerful 'batteries' in each of its pectoral fins. These batteries are honeycomb-like structures of prism-shaped cells filled with jelly. The ventral side of the fish is a negative electrode while the upper side is a positive electrode. Sea water completes the circuit, through which a substantial current passes. Any small fish which passes close to or touches the ray causes a reflex action which triggers an immediate electrical discharge. A fish caught in the path of this discharge is either killed or stunned and falls prey to the ray. I have heard it said that, anyone touching at the same time both upper and lower surface of a torpedo ray will get a shock comparable with that received from touching the sparking plug of a car when the engine is running. Even touching one side of a ray, which is lying on a wet deck, can cause a slight shock, although this does not occur if you are wearing rubber boots. Because of the danger of this electric discharge, every sea angler should learn to recognise a torpedo ray at sight. In the event of a catch, cut free your hook and tie on a new hook in place of the one left in the mouth of the fish. But do not throw your catch overboard! The record for this species is now open to claims.

Common Skate

This fish – occasionally referred to as a grey or blue skate – is, as its major name implies, the commonest of the three large skate and the one most frequently caught by anglers. Its colour is greyish-brown on the back, with light-coloured blotches and small dark spots; underside is grey, with dark streaks.

Common skate of well over 200 lb (90.7 kg) have been caught on rod and line. The largest recorded commercially-caught specimen weighed 400 lb (181.4 kg) and had a measured length of a little over 7 ft (2.1 m). Common skate are found all round the coast of Britain, although most come from Scottish and Irish waters.

Fenit, in Ireland, is a famous common-skate port; and at Ullapool, in western Ross, an annual skate-fishing championship takes place; and Scapa Flow, in the Orkney Islands, has recently produced a number of very big skate. If all goes well, it would seem likely that the common-skate record will change hands regularly from now on, for many of the known big-skate grounds are being fished for the first time ever. I have caught common skate over sand and gravel bottoms, but my best fish have always been hooked on rough mixed-ground. A big skate will eat practically anything edible it comes across, and an examination of the stomach contents of the large common skate I have caught, has produced the remains of crabs, lobsters, dogfish, pouting, mackerel and even small skate – proof that a big skate has a large and varied diet.

The last two giant skate I caught fell to coalfish. One skate weighed 158 lb (71.6 kg) the other 192 (87.1 kg). Both were caught off Orkney. In my opinion, the skate marks round these lovely northern isles are capable of producing fish well in excess of the current record.

Long-nosed Skate

This fish is easily recognisable by its abnormally-long snout. It is rather similar in colour to the common skate but it is smaller, rarely exceeding a length of 5 ft (1.5 m). It has a wide distribution and can be found over similar ground to the common skate. The few specimens I have hooked have always put up a better fight than common skate of similar size.

White Skate

The back of this fish is bluish-grey in colour, with paler spots which are very indistinct on the larger fish; underparts are very white. White skate are known to have reached a length of over 8 ft (2.4 m) and a weight of at least 500 lb (226.8 kg). A fish of such size would be a formidable creature to hook on rod and line. White skate can be regarded as a southern species; small specimens being very common off the coasts of Devon, Cornwall and Southern Ireland. Their feeding habits are similar to those of other large skate; they also inhabit similar ground.

Tackle

For the smaller species of ray, a 30 lb (13.6 kg) class hollow-glass boat rod should be used. Choice of reel depends on personal preference, but most anglers find that a multiplier suits their requirements. Although ray are not true fighting fish, their broad flat bodies, and their habit of spiralling up (against the pressure of the tide), make it impossible to catch them on really light lines. Because of this, most ray fishermen use a line with 30 lb (13.6 kg) breaking strain. All skates and rays have rough strong lips and, although it is possible to catch them on a nylon trace, it is advisable to use a wire link between reel line and hook. I have never actually known a ray to bite through a trace, but I *have* lost several fish when nylon traces snapped during the fight. On each occasion a careful examination of the point of breakage showed that the nylon had been crushed and flattened between the ray's lips. Choice of hook size for ray fishing depends on the fish you expect to catch and the bait you wish to use. Sting ray, for example, feed best on worm baits so a smallish hook is essential; my own choice being a size 2-0 stainless steel Model Perfect, a hook which is small enough to take a worm bait, but strong enough to withstand the strain of pumping up to the boat a fish which may well weigh 40 lb (18.2 kg) or more. The Model Perfect is, in fact, the only hook of this size that I can recommend for its strength, other makes of similar size having let me down by snapping at the bend, or straightening out under pressure. Hooks of this size should also be used for spotted and cuckoo ray: thornback, blonde, small-eyed ray, etc, prefer larger baits. Because of this, a larger hook must be used, a size 6-0 Model Perfect being ideal with fish fillet or squid-type baits. Model Perfects are narrower across the gape than most flat-forged hooks of similar size (see Fig. 68). This is a useful feature when ray are the quarry, for although most ray have largish mouths, the shape of the mouth is wide rather than deep. I believe, therefore, that a bait mounted on a hook with a narrow gape is more likely to be taken right away than one that is fastened to a wide-gape hook.

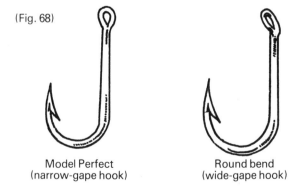

(Fig. 68)

| Model Perfect (narrow-gape hook) | Round bend (wide-gape hook) |

Big-skate tackle

Many a huge skate has been hooked and successfully boated on medium-weight tackle of the type already described. But for every huge skate caught a dozen break free and escape during the first few minutes of the fight. Fishing for big skate is a rough, tough occupation which calls for rugged tackle and a lot of skill. For years angling writers have described the fight of a big skate as 'like playing a tabletop on a sack of ballast'. From this I can only assume that these people have never hooked a really large specimen. For although skate seldom put up a spectacular fight, their sheer bulk and brute strength make them dour and formidable opponents. Most hooked skate cling to the sea bed using their huge bodies as a suction disc. These initial tactics make mincemeat out of normal boat tackle. Unless you happen to be fortunate enough to hook a big skate which keeps on the move, a medium boat-fishing outfit will not have the power to lift the fish from the sea bed without breaking under the tremendous strain. So I strongly advise anglers who intend to fish for big skate to buy an outfit strong enough to withstand the rigours of this type of angling. A hollow-glass rod of the shark type is essential. This should have a test curve of between 20 and 30 lb (9 and 13.6 kg). In other words it will reach its maximum curve when lifting a dead weight of 20 or 30 lb (9.1 or 13.6 kg) (see Fig. 69). Rods with either a full set of roller rings or a roller tip-ring and fully lined guard rings should be used. Good rings cut down friction and can save the angler considerable effort during a long hard fight. The best reel to use for big skate fishing is a large capacity multiplier. My own choice is the Grice and Young Tatler V, but a Penn reel of similar capacity would be just as good. The main reason for using a large capacity reel is so that it can be loaded with at least 300 yards (275 m) of heavy line – not that big skate take a great length of line on the run, but it is advisable to have plenty in reserve should a fish decide to run further than usual. Braided Terylene or Dacron of 50–60 lb (22.7–27.2 kg) should be used, bearing in mind that big skate of over 150 lb (68 kg) are fairly common in English, Irish and Scottish waters. I had a 192 lb (87 kg) skate, in Orkney on 60 lb (27.2 kg) line, that fought for over 20 minutes in a strong tide flow. On several occasions it had over 150 yards (137 m) of line off the reel.

Large skate, like most big fish, tend to be rather lazy, preferring one good meal to a lot of snacks. Because of this, it pays to use a generous amount of bait on a large hook. A whole large mackerel, or similar-sized fish, should be mounted on a size 8-0 or 10-0 hook, fastened by crimps to a 4 ft/m nylon-covered wire trace, which should have a minimum breaking strain of 60 lb (27.2 kg). This may sound unnecessarily strong: but you should bear in mind that, when a big skate is hooked, the trace will be in constant contact with the spiky rough skin and bony lips of the skate and will be subjected to considerable wear and tear before the fish is ready for the gaff. A strong barrel swivel should be used between trace and reel line. Do not use link swivels for this sort of heavy-duty work, as the wire link is a weak point that can easily break under the strain.

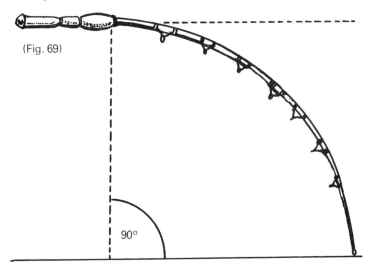

(Fig. 69)

90°

Test curve of rod = pull needed to bend rod through quarter circle

Methods

A running leger is the only practical form of terminal tackle to use for skate and ray of all types and sizes. These fish are, by nature of their shape, obviously bottom feeders. To be successful the bait must be anchored right on the sea bed. Skate are sluggish, inactive fish which seldom chase after their food, preferring to wander slowly across the bottom picking up any edible object they can find. To work properly, a leger intended for skate should carry enough weight to anchor it in one position. Long flowing traces are not necessary. Most successful anglers use the trace swivel as a stop for the lead (see Fig. 70). Anglers have recently discovered that skate are attracted to the blade of

an artificial spoon, and some good catches have been taken on
normal leger tackle to which a swivel and spoon blade has been
added (see Fig. 71). Skate probably see the spoon blade as a
small fish, which they attempt to catch, the bait itself being
located the moment they drop on to the spoon.

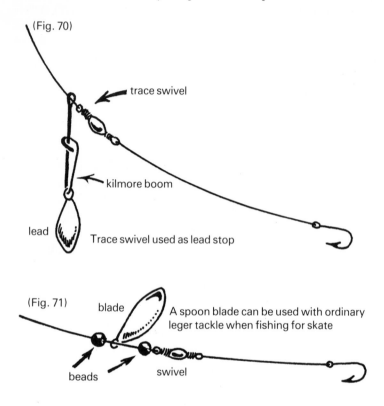

(Fig. 70)

trace swivel

kilmore boom

lead

Trace swivel used as lead stop

(Fig. 71) blade A spoon blade can be used with ordinary
leger tackle when fishing for skate

beads swivel

Bites

Skate bites follow a very definite pattern. Unfortunately, many
anglers strike at the first indication of a bite. This may be fine
for a number of fish but a premature strike during a skate-
fishing session will only lead to lost fish. It is essential to sit back
and ignore the preliminary bite indications, so giving the fish
time to take the bait right inside its mouth. The first pull on the
rod tip is not a bite at all; it is caused by the skate flopping down
on top of the bait and line. A strike at this stage will simply whip
the bait out from under the body of the fish and, in all proba-

bility, put it off feed for the remainder of the day. To avoid this, the first bites should be left to develop. Once the fish has taken the bait well inside its mouth, it will move, pulling the rod tip slowly down as it goes. This is the time – and the only time – to attempt to set your hook. Most of the smaller skates and rays swim with the tide when they move away with a bait. Very big skate usually swim against the tide causing the line to fall slack as they go. This slackening is a clear indication that the fish can be struck; and a fair warning that you have caught a big fish. The luckiest angler I ever saw was a man fishing off the Hampshire coast who had this type of bite, did not realise what he had and let the fish wind the line twice round the boat's anchor rope: by all the laws of fishing, that should have been the end of the matter, but the line held long enough for the fish to work its way up the rope to the surface: then, in full view of everyone in the boat, the great fish swam twice round the rope, unwound the line and was gaffed as it cruised past the side of the boat. When weighed, it tipped the scales at exactly 100 lb (45.3 kg). Playing a big skate is often a long and exhausting job. First the fish has to be coaxed off the seabed, then it has to be played against the tide. Under no circumstances should it be allowed to get its head down. If it does, the flow of water pressing down on its angled body, coupled with its own weight and muscle strength, will be enough to break the line. I have seen several big skate lost right on the surface, simply because the angler relaxed for a second and let fish get its head down. More rods are broken per annum by big skate than by any other species; but, providing an angler is willing to play skate carefully, these breakages should never occur. A shoulder harness and a belt-type rod bucket are worth buying if you seriously intend to take up big-skate hunting.

Shore fishing

Most skate and ray are caught from boats. Three species, the thornback, the small-eyed ray and the sting ray are also commonly caught by shore fishermen. Thornback are caught mainly from beaches on single-hook legers, baited with fish-head or fillet. Small-eyed ray are more of a fish for rock anglers. In West Country waters, where sand patches are found within reasonable casting range of rocks, fishing for small-eyed ray has developed into something of a cult. Top bait is fresh sand eel:

135

stale baits catch very little. Night fishing produces the most action, and on a good night, when the ray are active, this style of angling can be both exciting and productive. Sting ray may not be your idea of fun, but a good many south and east coast anglers specialise in these odd-looking ray. Worm or crab make the best baits for sting-ray fishing. A warm sultry evening, an incoming tide and no wind are the ideal conditions. I have caught sting ray in excess of 40 lb (18.1 kg) and can testify to their fighting ability when hooked. In the shallow Solent area, I have even seen a hooked sting ray attempt to jump.

A word of warning

Never attempt to extract a hook from the mouth of a big skate by hand. The crushing power of its rasp-like lips can easily pulp unwary fingers. The thrashing spiky tail of a large skate should also be avoided, as it can inflict a painful blow. Finally, be very careful of the claspers of male skate (see Fig. 72). These contain a sharp bony plate which can cause a nasty cut.

Although this chapter covers skate and ray fishing, I feel that two other fish are worth mentioning as they are often found over similar ground.

(Fig. 72)

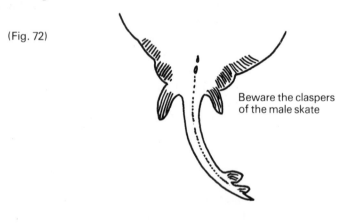

Beware the claspers
of the male skate

Monkfish

Monkfish are the direct link between the shark and the skate families. They are often confused with angler fish, even though the two species bear little resemblance to one another. The

136

monkfish is usually greyish-brown in colour. The average weight of a rod-caught monkfish is somewhere between 25–45 lb (11.3–20.4 kg), but specimens up to 60 lb (27.2 kg) are by no means rare. Monkfish have a wide distribution but are commonest in the southern half of the Channel. Large ones are commonly caught off the south-west coast of Ireland. They are ungainly creatures incapable of showing any great turn of speed.

To catch their food they fan the seabed vigorously with their fins and then eat the small fish that are attracted by the cloudy water. Practically anything that swims and is small enough will be eaten by hungry monkfish but small flatfish seem to form their main diet. Monkfish are great scavengers and will eat any dead fish they find, irrespective of whether it is stale or fresh. Despite their large average size and bulky thick-set appearance, monkfish seldom put up much resistance when hooked. I have known the odd specimen to fight really hard but this is unusual.

Most professionals dislike monkfish and consider them dangerous to handle. In this respect I agree with them. A big monk has formidable tooth-filled jaws and the unpleasant habit of suddenly lunging forward, snapping its mouth open and shut as it goes.

Angler Fish

This is probably the ugliest species of fish on the British list, with a huge head and sharply tapering body which makes it easy to identify. Like the monkfish, the angler fish is a spring and summer visitor which spends the winter months in deep water well offshore.

Angler fish have a wide distribution and have been recorded from all parts of the British Isles. They turn up in the most unusual places. Confirmed bottom feeders, they live almost entirely on fish. Owing to their grotesque shape, angler fish have to rely on ambushing their food, for they are incapable of fast bursts of speed and are, therefore, unable to pursue and catch prey. Instead, nature has furnished them with a strip of skin attached to the end of the first ray of the dorsal fin. This strip is used as a lure, to attract small fish to within striking range of an angler's huge tooth-filled mouth, hence the name angler fish. The fin ray, which acts as a fishing rod, is long enough to be inclined forward, right over the fish's mouth; there can be little doubt that an angler fish activates its lure to make it more attractive to the shoals of food fish. Very occasionally, angler fish will rise to the surface and try to engulf a sleeping sea bird. Like cod, the angler fish will swallow all sorts of trash from the seabed. Jam jars, tins, sea weights, lumps of scrap metal, corks and bits of wood have all been found in the stomach of these fish. Although it cannot be classed as a true fighting fish, the bulk of a big angler makes it a formidable opponent to tackle. The two that I caught felt just like weed-filled sacks and on both occasions I was not at all sure that I had, in fact, hooked a fish until the creatures surfaced. In recent seasons, some huge angler fish have been taken by anglers fishing close to wartime wrecks, and I feel that the next record for the species will be taken from a wreck mark.

Tope

The tope, a small member of the shark family, is very popular with anglers in most parts of the British Isles, and there is an official tope club in Britain. To become a member of the tope club, it is necessary to catch a tope of over 30 lb (13.6 kg) on rod and line. Each year this club awards a number of trophies for the best fish of the season.

The tope has a typically shark-like appearance, with two dorsal fins and prominent gill slits. Its big tail has a deeply notched upper lobe, and the fish has a grey or greyish-brown back and white underparts. The average weight of a rod-caught tope is about 30 lb (13.6 kg), but fish of 45 lb (20.4 kg) are by no means exceptional. The record rod-caught specimen weighed over 70 lb (31.7 kg), a fair indication that tope can reach a large size. The largest tope I ever caught weighed 64 lb (29 kg) and came from a deep hole inside Strangford Lough in Northern Ireland. This lough is, in my opinion, the most likely place in Europe to produce the new record for this species.

Contrary to the popular belief that tope are confined to Britain's south and south-western coastline, they have a wide distribution. They are very common in the Wash and some large catches are taken annually from this area. Further north, they are rarely caught, until one gets as far as Scotland. In Luce Bay and around the Scottish islands, these fish are often very common, and it would seem that they can be caught almost anywhere around Great Britain, provided that anglers are prepared to fish for them with the right baits and tackle. In recent years, several Welsh ports have consistently made news with tope catches, proof, indeed, that these fish are more common than people imagine them to be. Tope are a summer species with the best catches being made during the four month period from June until the end of September. Where I live, on the Hampshire coast, the first tope catches are made about mid May, with June and July being the most productive months. During the past two seasons, however, large tope have been caught during December and January on baits intended for cod. As yet, it is impossible to say whether these are freak captures, or whether tope are present in the area throughout the whole of the year. I am fairly sure that time will show us that some tope do stay close to the shore the whole year round. Taken on an overall basis, tope can be classed as game fish; for although everyone does encounter the odd specimen on rod and line that gives up without a struggle, the majority put up a determined battle. Probably the best catch of tope ever taken off the Hampshire coast was the one, I and a party of friends, made during early June 1965 when we took 750 lb (340 kg) of tope. The smallest fish weighed 32 lb 9 oz (14.75 kg) and the largest 54 lb 8 oz (24.7 kg). All the fish were caught less than a mile from the shore on a mark 35 ft (10.6 m) deep.

Practically every large tope caught is female; the males seldom weigh more than 30 lb (13.6 kg). Tope have become increasingly scarce along the south coast of England in recent years, due, no doubt, to the fact that almost every tope caught in the past has been killed. I never cease to be surprised that anglers, who should know better, still make a point of destroying each tope they catch, in the mistaken belief that they are helping the other fish by killing the predators which feed on them. Without fish like tope to keep some sort of natural balance, small sea fish quickly overbreed, with the result that they exhaust the food supplies of a given area and, being half-starved, become stunted.

I make a point of returning tope alive to the water, whenever possible; although there can be no objection to anglers retaining the odd large tope for competition purposes. Far too many of these grand fish finish up in the dustbin or under rose beds, and I think it is about time that sea anglers came to their senses and, with an eye to sport in the future, returned the bulk of the tope alive to the sea.

Tackle

Rods

To my knowledge, the only rod specifically designed for tope fishing was the Jack Hargreaves Tope Rod, manufactured by the now defunct company of Davenport & Fordham. These rods are now collectors items, treasured by their owners and lusted after by less fortunate anglers. My own Hargreaves has accounted for hundreds of big fish, from tope to blue shark and ton-up skate. Nowadays anglers use rods designed for line class fishing. The ideal tope rod being a 30 lb (13.6 kg) class weapon. For shore fishing, a beachcaster in the 6–8 oz (0.17–0.226 kg) range is ideal. This may sound heavy, but when casting a beach rod for tope fishing it is essential to take into account the size of the bait being used.

Reels

A medium-sized multiplying reel, capable of holding 300 yards (275 m) or more of 30 lb (13.6 kg) breaking-strain line will do admirably for all aspects of tope fishing. There are many serviceable patterns available. For boat fishing, the Tatler 2½-0, the Mitchell 624 and the Penn Mariner are the three most serviceable reels I have used. For beach work, a Penn Squidder or Abu 700 are perfect; both have ample capacity and both are designed for long casting.

Lines

There is no necessity to use extra-strong line for tope fishing. Provided that your reel holds 300 yards (275 m) of line with a 25–30 lb (11.3–13.6 kg) breaking strain and the star drag is set correctly, any tope you encounter round British coasts can be easily beaten. I have had several tope in the 50 lb (22.7 kg) class over the years; and although I have known a fish to run out over 150 yards (137 m) during the initial stages of the battle, I have always found that they burn themselves out long before the 200 yard (182 m) mark is reached and can be turned and pumped back to the boat without ever having run out all the reel line. From my own experience with tope, I cannot credit the stories I hear of fish running out 300 yards (275 m) or more without stopping.

For tope fishing from a boat a braided Dacron line is much better than a monofilament line. The stretch in a long length of nylon makes it very difficult to maintain constant contact with a running fish. Braided line does not stretch, so there is no danger of losing contact during the time the fish is pulling against the line. For beachcasting a line with a maximum breaking strain of 25 lb (11.3 kg) should be used. Where ultra-long casting is essential, this breaking strain can be dropped to 18 lb (8.2 kg). On the north Cornish coastline, where large tope are sought-after by rock fishermen, the local experts use a line with 15 lb (6.8 kg) breaking strain and still stop and subdue quite heavy fish. It takes a good angler to stop a big fish on line as light as this, and I would not advise a beginner to try it.

Hooks and traces

No two tope fishermen ever agree on the size of hook and length of trace needed for tope fishing. Some swear by extra-long traces; others are equally convinced that a short trace will suffice. Choice of hook size depends on the type and size of the bait you intend to use. I am afraid that, in this respect, the average sea angler lags a long way behind the average fresh-water angler, who has learned from an early age that it is essential to use the right combination of bait and hook size at all times. I have often seen sea anglers hooking a whole herring or mackerel on a size 2-0 hook in the fond belief that one hook will do for small or large baits.

For small soft baits such as fish fillet or imported squid, a size 6-0 stainless steel Model Perfect hook is ideal. For whole fish baits, used either alive or dead, an 8-0 or even 10-0 hook should be used. Tope have big mouths and although a 10-0 hook may look enormous in the hand it does not look over-big in the mouth of a good-size tope. When tope fishing from the shore, small baits of the sand-eel type should be fished on carefully sharpened 2-0 or 4-0 hooks. Forged hooks are best for this sort of fishing. I would advise anglers to use a trace of 2-3 ft (0.6-0.9 m). Traces of 5-7 ft (1.5-2.1 m) may keep the rough skin of the tope away from the reel line, but they are pretty unmanageable, particularly when made up of nylon-covered wire which, in long lengths, tends to twist and kink with the movement of the bait in the water. I have never lost a tope through using a shortish wire trace, although I have lost fish through faulty wire.

Tope are bottom feeders, quite content to pick up an easy meal in the shape of a freshly-dead fish or a fish fillet. Tope are also very fond of squid or cuttlefish. In the Solent area, local anglers say that the first sign of tope being present is when they find cuttlefish bodies, minus the heads, floating on the surface. I would say that the vast majority of rod-caught tope fall to mackerel or herring baits; although almost any small fish can be used for tope catching. My favourite tope bait is pouting, which I use alive or dead. I have caught tope on small haddock, wrasse and gurnard in Scotland, and it seems to me that providing a bait is fresh, tope are extremely catholic in their tastes. I am sure that if more anglers used live baits for tope fishing far more big tope would be caught.

Live baits should be hooked once through the wrist of the tail. This gives a firm hook-hold without killing the bait. Dead baits can be hooked in a similar fashion or through both lips. Fillet baits should be tied to the shank and eye of the hook, otherwise water pressure will cause them to slide down and bunch on the bend of the hook. A bait that does this will rarely catch tope. A fresh mackerel with its head removed makes a first-class tope bait. The hook should be passed through the wrist of the tail and lashed to the thick end of the bait with thread or wool. For shore fishing sand eels make excellent bait.

Handling

Provided that a hooked tope is played out carefully and firmly, it can usually be brought up to the side of the boat. Once there, it is ready to be pulled inboard. At this stage, it can be gaffed or tailed, depending on whether it is to be retained or released. Modern sea anglers now tail most of the tope they catch, to avoid damaging them with the gaff point. Tailing is simple enough if one keeps cool and gets a firm grip on the hard wrist of the tail. Once this is done, and the tail is out of the water, the fish will be practically powerless. It can then be dragged or lifted over the gunwale. To avoid harming the fish, it should be lifted by the tail and dorsal fin. Failing this, it can be pulled bodily over the side. This method tends to rupture the fish so the tail and dorsal fin technique is the best method to employ. Once the fish is safely inboard, the hook can be removed or, if it is well inside the mouth, the trace can be cut, leaving the hook embedded in the flesh. The tope can then be weighed, photographed and released intact. Tope should not be picked up by the tail only if this can be avoided. When hanging head down, the stomach sometimes drops forward and ruptures so badly that the fish dies, even if it seems to swim strongly when returned to the water. For weighing purposes, the hook of the spring balance should be carefully inserted in one of the gill slits so that the fish hangs tail downwards. For photographs, the fish should be held supported by both hands. Take care to avoid the jaws, which snap automatically every time something touches them. Some people like to eat tope steaks, though tope cannot really be classed as a very edible species. My advice is to return all fish caught to the water.

Methods

Tope are bottom feeders. Consequently, to be successful a bait must be presented on or close to the sea bed. A plain running leger is the most practical terminal tackle to use and this gear accounts for over 90% of the tope caught each year.

I am convinced that tope are attracted by movement and, to a lesser extent, by smell. Live baits will naturally provide their own movement to help attract prowling tope. Dead baits or fish-fillet baits, on the other hand, can be fished in several different ways. At present, the most widely used method is to stop the lead 8 or 10 ft (2.4 or 3 m) from the bait, using a length of valve rubber on a matchstick, hitched to the line as a stop. This will allow the bait to waver about with the tide in an attractive fashion. When fishing alone or with one or two other anglers, this idea can be enlarged on by lowering the baited hook over the stern of the boat and letting it drift away with the tide. The lead and sliding tackle should be held in the hand until about 20-30 ft (6-9.1 m) line is out, then a stop (made from a short length of bicycle-valve rubber) should be hitched to the line to prevent the weight from sliding down to the trace. Once this stop is in place, the lead can be lowered in the normal way until it reaches the bottom, where the bait is free to flow about in a wide arc beyond the lead. When a fish is hooked and the lead weight comes up against the top ring of the rod, the pressure will cause the valve-rubber stop to double up so that it passes through the eye of the sliding boom and releases the lead, which will then slide down to the trace swivel and allow the fish to be brought up on a short length of line. A thin sliver of matchstick can also be used, but it must be thin enough to snap under strain, so that it releases the lead correctly without jamming up the tackle. An equally effective, although not widely used method, is to use a 5-6 ft (1.5-1.8 m) length of line between hook and weight, and trot the bait out over the seabed so that it covers as much ground as possible. To fish this tackle properly, it is essential to achieve the correct balance of terminal gear. The lead should be just heavy enough to hold bottom and light enough to roll every time the rod tip is lifted and line allowed to run out. This is the most successful technique to use in strong tides.

For shore fishing, shorter trace lengths must be used, otherwise casting distance will be cut to an unacceptable degree. A maximum trace length of 2 ft 6 in (0.76 m) should be used for this style of fishing.

Using float tackle

Float fishing for tope is a shallow-water boat-fishing method that I have found to work extremely well. This method is only practicable during slack-tide periods, but when conditions are right, it can be a most rewarding and exciting form of angling. Basically, this method is a scaled-down adaptation of the technique used to catch shark on float-fished baits; the float, of course, being smaller. I use a plastic detergent bottle as a float, but there are several large-sized sliding sea-floats that are also suitable for this work. The most important point to remember when setting up this tackle is that tope are bottom feeders, so the bait must be fished on or just off the seabed

Let us say, for example, that a tope mark is 30 ft (13.6 m) deep. Which means that the float stop should be set about 5 ft (1.5 m) more than the known depth of water, to allow for drag, etc. Under normal circumstances, lead should not be used to weight the bait down. If, however, the tide is running fairly rapidly it pays to use a 1½ oz (0.04 kg) barrel lead on the line, just above the trace swivel. This should be sufficient to take the bait down and keep it close to the bottom. It may be necessary in really hard tides to set the float at 15 ft (4.6 m) more than the depth of the water, to allow for additional water pressure on the bait, which tends to lift it off the seabed. All things being equal, this method can be fished quite easily from an anchored boat.

A braided line should be used for this style of tope fishing, because, being fairly buoyant in itself, it will tend to stay close to the surface as the bait is worked away from the boat. This is important. A sunken line between rod tip and float can lead to all sorts of complications. Bad tangles become inevitable, and direct striking at a taking fish becomes an impossibility, due to pressure of water on the sunken line. The boat can be allowed to drift when the tide is barely moving, so that the bait gradually covers several miles of ground. This is only advisable when the bottom is comparatively snag free, otherwise the bait will continually catch on underwater obstructions. For float fishing for tope, a large bait seems to produce the best results. I usually use a whole mackerel or herring, hooked once through the root of the tail so that it trips along head down over the bottom. Fishing for tope in this manner calls for a considerable amount of concentration. The moment a fish pulls the float under, it is essential to snap the reel out of gear so that the running fish can take line as it moves away. Tope are not timid biters, but they quickly drop a bait if they suspect all is not well. Strangely enough, the drag on the float does not appear to worry them; but a slight pull from the rod tip will often cause them to eject the bait immediately.

I find that most of the tope I catch follow a definite pattern. First comes the actual taking of the bait. This is normally a fairly savage affair. It would seem that as a general rule, the fish actually snap up the bait on the run. Because of this the float either disappears with a crash or races away over the surface, submerging as it goes. To ensure that there are no snags at this initial stage, it is essential to hold the rod at all times. Once the float has gone and the reel spool is revolving at speed, the angler must not strike until the fish either begins to slow down, which it usually does, or it becomes obvious that it is not going to stop. In either event, the reel should be put back into gear and, as the line pulls tight, the rod lifted steadily back over the shoulder. Heavy strikes should be avoided, otherwise a breakage may occur.

Dogfish

Few boat anglers enjoy catching dogfish. Apart from being good make-weight for competition anglers, they tend to be regarded as vermin by the rest. The bull huss is the largest of the two common dogfish, a big, greedy fish which can easily exceed a weight of 20 lb (9 kg). Bull huss are reddish-brown in colour, with large dark blotches. They are commonest over rough ground, often frequenting good conger marks. They can be caught during the day, but in my experience they feed best after dark. I have caught many large specimens, on various conger marks in the Channel and while fishing off the north coast of Cornwall. The lesser-spotted dogfish, which seldom attains any great size, lives mainly on sandy ground and makes a great nuisance of itself by taking baits intended for better fish. It is similar in colour to the bull huss except that, instead of being covered in large blotches, its spots are small and very neat. Both fish have the unpleasant habit of wrapping themselves round an unwary hand and then slowly unwinding – the sandpaper-like texture of their skin causing nasty abrasions. It is, therefore, advisable to take care when handling them.

Dogfish are caught mainly by boat anglers, although bull huss are occasionally taken at night by rock anglers. Dogfish are opportunists, and fish, worm and shellfish baits can all be used to catch them. Neither type put up much of a struggle when hooked, although a good-sized bull huss taken on a beach-casting outfit can give a little sport.

Spurdog

The spurdog is similar in outward appearance to the tope and many novice anglers confuse the two. Although adult specimens grow to $3\frac{1}{2}$-4 ft (1.06-1.2 m) in length they do not reach the size of tope. When handling spurdog, great care should be taken to avoid the claw-like spine on the dorsal fin. Spurdog are normally found in packs and are, therefore, very popular with competition anglers; once a pack is located the fish can be caught two or three at a time until a large total weight is amassed. From the sporting point of view, however, spurdog are of little interest because they are easily caught and put up very little fight when hooked.

Unlike most of their tribe, spurdog do not confine their activities to the bottom alone. They are quite content to feed at any level, so long as they can get an ample supply of food. A pack of hungry spurdog will take any bait an angler cares to use, and the majority of anglers regard spurdog as bait-robbing scavengers. They have a novelty value the first time a pack is encountered but the continual catching of fish soon begins to pall. Although the best way to catch spurdog is to leger a fish-fillet bait, a string of baited mackerel feathers, or single or double-hook paternoster rigs, can also be used to good effect. Spurdog will strike at artificial baits, and I have had some big catches of these fish while using pirk baits for cod, coalfish and pollack. An artificial lure can be made more attractive by the addition of a sliver of fish or squid strip.

Smooth-hound

In recent years, smooth-hound have become something of a cult fish. Many articles have been written about them, particularly by east-coast anglers, many of whom appear to have become addicted to these fish. The smooth-hound fights harder than any other member of the dogfish clan. In general appearance the adult smooth-hound is very similar to a small tope. It does not, however, have the graceful shape of the tope and its fins are rather large in comparison to its body. Adult specimens are grey on the back with white underparts. The starry smooth-hound have a freckling of white spots on their back. Two local names for this fish are 'ray-mouthed dogfish' and 'skate-toothed shark'. Instead of having proper teeth, its lips are covered with hard slabs, similar to those of a skate or ray. Smooth-hound up to 5 ft (1.5 m) long have been caught by commercial fishermen and I have seen specimens to over 20 lb (9 kg) caught on rod and line.

Like most of the dogfish family, the smooth-hound is a con-firmed bottom feeder but, unlike other dogfish, it rarely eats fish, preferring to feed on worms, crabs, etc. Large smooth-hound are very common in the Solent and off the Essex marks, where they are usually caught during the summer months on leger-tackle baited with ragworm or hermit-crab tails. On lightish tackle, a large smooth-hound can be relied upon to put up a good struggle. Size for size its fighting ability is similar to that of the tope.

Smooth-hound feed best during sultry weather, and most of my largest catches have been made in the late evening. Unlike tope, which are bold biters, smooth-hound normally play with a bait for some time before taking it into their mouths. Because of this habit, it is advisable to ignore preliminary bite indications, and wait until the fish moves away with the bait, before attempting to strike – otherwise you will just pull the hook and bait from the lips of the smooth-hound. A freshly caught smooth-hound makes excellent eating; being boneless, it is easy to clean and cut up.

Wrasse

Five or six species of wrasse are found around the coast of the British Isles, but only two of them are of any interest to the angler. These, in order of importance are the ballan wrasse and the cuckoo wrasse. Wrasse are adapted for life among rocks and heavy tides, and cuckoo wrasse are often common on offshore grounds, particularly in the lower half of the Channel. At one time, the male and female cuckoo wrasse were thought to be separate species owing to the difference in their colour. The male fish is orange-yellow, with a dark blue patch on the head and two blue stripes running from the gill covers almost to the root of the tail. The female fish is drab in comparison, but is still a most-attractive fish, pink on the back; with pale underparts and three dark spots just under the dorsal fin. Maximum length for both fish is about 12 in (0.3 m).

The largest and most interesting member of the wrasse family is the ballan, a fish which can reach a weight of approximately 10 lb (4.5 kg). The ballan wrasse has a deep solid-looking body, a long spiky dorsal fin and neat, strong white teeth. Its coloration is extremely variable, the commonest colours being brown or greeny-brown. The belly and head of the adult fish are often netted with red or orange-red scales, each of which has a light centre spot. Occasionally, very large green specimens are caught; these, in my experience, are fairly rare.

The average weight of a rod-caught ballan wrasse is $1\frac{1}{2}$-4 lb (0.7-1.8 kg), but far larger fish exist. My largest wrasse, for example, tipped the scales at $9\frac{3}{4}$ lb (4.4 kg) and I have also had several other fish of over 7 lb (3.2 kg). All my large wrasse came before the terrible freeze-up during the winter of 1962-1963. The intense cold of that period killed the wrasse in vast quantities and it is only now that the fish are becoming re-established in any quantity. During 1968 the old record for wrasse was removed from the record list. At present the record is held by a 8 lb 6 oz (3.8 kg) fish. Prior to the winter of 1962–1963 this would have been an easy record to smash; but as things stand, it may be some years before a larger fish is caught.

Unfortunately, wrasse are still regarded as vermin by many anglers and most of the fish caught are killed out of hand, with no thought for the future. This is a tragic state of affairs. My advice would be to return all wrasse to the sea. They do no harm whatsoever and, on the right tackle, they provide excellent sport. There is no valid reason for killing them.

Tackle

To get the best out of wrasse fishing, it pays to fish as light as possible. Nothing special is required, bass-strength gear being ideal for general wrasse fishing. Make no mistake, however, a ballan wrasse hooked on lightish tackle is a hard-fighting fish, so don't fish too light a line, or you will lose more fish than you land.

Baits

Wrasse live mainly on crustacea, molluscs and marine worms; the best baits being limpets, prawns, worms and crabs. Hard-backed crabs the size of a tenpenny piece are ideal. I catch more wrasse on live crabs than on dead ones, and the method I use to attach them to the hook is as follows. Turn the crab over on its back; push the hook point firmly through the triangle at the base of its shell, making sure that the point and barb of the hook protrude through the crab's back. Hard-backed crabs hooked in this fashion remain alive and attractive to fish for long periods. Hard-backed crabs are easy to collect in quantity, and half an hour spent turning over rocks at low tide should yield more than enough bait-sized crab for a whole day's fishing. Big wrasse will also eat live fish. I have had several good specimens while live-baiting with tiny rock fish, and have also had some fair wrasse on live sand eels. Ballan wrasse do not respond well to fish strip bait; cuckoo wrasse, on the other hand, prefer a strip of squid or fish to all other baits. The reason for this is that cuckoo wrasse are an offshore species and are not accustomed to seeing small crabs, prawns or worms in any quantity.

A large earthworm makes an excellent wrasse bait and is just as potent as a marine worm. Wrasse have large mouths, so baits should be fished on size 1 or 2 hooks (freshwater scale).

Methods

Wrasse are basically a rock-haunting species, and although they sometimes feed directly from the seabed, I find it pays to suspend the bait 12-18 in (0.3-0.46 m) off the bottom. The best terminal tackle is a single-hook nylon paternoster, and I make mine up so that the bait is suspended roughly 15 in (0.38 m) above the seabed. This keeps the bait out of reach of hungry shore crabs and also allows it to waver about with the tide. Even more important, it keeps the bait suspended in the thick 'soup' of broken weed, dead shellfish, crabs, etc, that wash back and forth with the tide. Wrasse are attracted to this natural ground-bait, and when they find a bait suspended among all the other edible matter, they take with the utmost confidence. Never use a two-hook paternoster over a mark where large ballan wrasse are known to feed, for wrasse feed in groups and, more often than not, you will hook two fish at once, and if this happens a breakage is almost certain. Despite their unfounded reputation for being poor fighters, big wrasse are powerful fish and their first power dive for freedom can be difficult to check; two fish hooked and going in different directions are practically impossible to stop, so take my advice and use only one hook.

Silver Eel

Anglers who do a lot of fishing in estuaries or large harbours often catch silver (freshwater) eels. Although these tend to be small, it is possible to catch some fine specimens when they pass through the estuaries on their way out to the open sea during the breeding migration. These migration runs usually occur in the late spring or autumn months. The silver eel is a common river eel which has spent most of its life in freshwater. When the urge to breed strikes, the eels forsake the freshwater and make their way down to the sea via any suitable waterway they can find. During the autumn migration, hundreds of good-sized eels come down the rivers each day and the silver eel fishing can be very good indeed.

Tackle

Nothing elaborate is required to catch silver eels, and to get the best out of these fish it is advisable to fish as light as possible. Wrasse-strength tackle is perfect. As silver eels feed mainly on the bottom, a running-leger rig should be used. Some anglers use a plain nylon trace but I much prefer plain braided wire with a breaking strain of about 10 lb (4.5 kg). I use this wire because I know from past experience that the sharp little teeth of a big eel can easily chafe a nylon trace. I do not believe in using an extra-long length of wire trace for silver eel, as I find that the stiffness of a long wire trace will sometimes cause eel to drop the bait. Because of this, I make up my eel traces in two sections. First, a 2 ft (0.6 m) section of nylon, of similar breaking strain to the wire, on each end of which I tie a link swivel. Second, I attach an 8 in (20 cm) length of wire to one of these swivels, to the end of which I fasten the hook. A suitably-sized sliding bomb-shaped lead is then run directly on to the reel line, and the loose trace swivel is used to join the trace and the reel line together. The swivel also acts as a stop for the running lead. Hooks should range from size 1 to size 2-0, depending on the size and type of bait being used. Silver eels are confirmed meat eaters and will pick up any fresh meat bait they can find. Both marine and earthworms make good eel baits. Many anglers, however, prefer to use cuttings taken from the back, sides or belly of a fresh fish. Eels are not fussy. Provided that the bait is fresh, almost any dead fish can be turned into bait. At one time or another I have known eels to take a variety of baits, including raw rabbit meat, white bacon fat and liver.

Although scavengers, eels are cautious feeders and will eject any bait which arouses their suspicion. Because of this, the rod should be held at all times, so that loose line can be paid out the moment an eel picks up the bait. This is important, for all silver eels have a habit of picking up a bait and running off with it without swallowing it. If they feel any drag during this initial run, they simply drop the bait. If they can run out line, however, they will soon stop and begin to swallow the bait properly. To make absolutely certain of hooking the eel on the strike it is advisable to wait for it to run off a second time before attempting to set the hook.

Horse Mackerel

During the summer months, horse mackerel (or scad) are extremely common in many areas. Many anglers regard them as vermin. I keep a more open mind about scad for, if nothing else, they make good bait for larger fish. To the untrained eye, the scad bears a superficial resemblance to the true mackerel; but the huge eye of the scad and the sharp bony ridge on its side make it an easy-enough fish to identify. Although not as game as the true mackerel, a large scad hooked on light tackle will give a good account of itself, particularly when hooked in deepish water. Scad can be caught by any of the methods used for mackerel, with fish cuttings, worms and sand eels making the best natural baits.

Gurnard

Although there are six British and Irish gurnards, only three are commonly caught by boat anglers. These are the grey, red and tub gurnard. All three are strange-looking fish, their heads being large and square, their bodies narrow and sharply tapered. They have two dorsal fins, the first one being very spiny. The ventral fins are large in comparison with the overall size of the fish and there are six leg-like feelers projecting from the throat. These are used to locate food. The grey gurnard, as its name implies, is a dull-coloured fish; but the red and tub gurnards are almost tropical in coloration, both being bright red. The tub gurnard is easy to distinguish, however, for it has vivid blue margins on its pectoral fins. Tub gurnard reach a weight of at least 10 lb (4.5 kg). Gurnards have a wide distribution, and I have caught specimens from Scottish sea lochs, from Irish waters and from marks in the Channel. Fish-strip bait, presented on leger or paternoster gear, should be used to catch them. Great care must be taken when handling these spiky fish, as their numerous spines can inflict painful cuts and scratches, although not actually poisonous.

Weever

Each year a number of anglers are taken to hospital after catching and handling weever fish. Strangely enough, few anglers realise just how dangerous these can be. Of the two British varieties, the lesser weever is the most poisonous; but the greater weever is also an ugly customer if picked up by inexperienced hands. Both fish have a poisonous sac situated directly underneath the first spine of the dorsal fin. This spine is hollow. When a weever is picked up and held firmly the sharp spine penetrates the angler's skin. At the same time, the pressure on the spine pushes the poison sac down and a jet of poison flows up through the spine into the angler's blood stream. In extreme cases, this venom has caused death: more normally, it gives the victim a few days of very unpleasant pain. There is a similar poison sac and spine situated on the fish's gill covers. In my opinion, the only way to deal with a weever is to cut the trace above the hook and let the fish go.

Both weevers are very similar in outward appearance having mottled drab brown bodies and pug-nosed faces. The lesser weever seldom reaches a length of more than 7 in (17.5 cm) but the greater weever can measure at least 16 in (0.4 m).

Most of the weevers I have caught were taken on worm baits, but they will also take fish strips and shellfish baits.

Index

Numbers in *italic* refer to the numbered colour illustrations in the colour section.

157